P9-CLX-663

how to do
just about
anything
with your
digital photos

how to do
just about
anything
with your
digital photos

- digital scrapbooking
- image enhancement
- creative projects
- web and e-mail sharing

graham davis

Reader's Digest

The Reader's Digest Association, Inc.
Pleasantville, New York/Montreal

contents

A READER'S DIGEST BOOK

This edition published by The Reader's Digest Association
by arrangement with
THE ILEX PRESS LIMITED
The Old Candlemakers
West Street, Lewes
East Sussex, BN7 2NZ, U.K.

For Ilex Press
Publisher Alastair Campbell
Executive Publisher Sophie Collins
Creative Director Peter Bridgewater
Editorial Director Steve Luck
Design Manager Tony Seddon
Editor Ben Renow-Clarke
Designer Ginny Zeal

For Reader's Digest
U.S. Project Editor David Schiff
Canadian Project Editor Pamela Johnson
Executive Editor, Trade Publishing Dolores York
Designer George McKeon
Director, Trade Publishing Christopher T. Reggio
Vice President & Publisher, Trade Publishing Harold Clarke

Library of Congress Cataloging-in-Publication Data

Davis, Graham, 1946–
    How to do just about anything with your digital photos :
digital scrapbooking, image enhancement, creative projects,
Web and e-mail sharing / Graham Davis
    p. cm
ISBN 0-7621-0493-7
    1. Photographs—Conservation and restoration—Data
processing. 2. Photography—Digital techniques. 4. Scrapbooks—
Data processing. 5. Digital preservation. I. Title

TR465.D39 2005
775—dc22

                        2004050829

Address any comments about
How to Do Just about Anything with Your Digital Photos to:
The Reader's Digest Association, Inc.
Adult Trade Publishing
Reader's Digest Road
Pleasantville, NY 10570-7000

For more Reader's Digest products and information,
visit our website:
www.rd.com (in the United States)
www.readersdigest.ca (in Canada)
www.readersdigest.com.au (in Australia)

Printed by Hong Kong Graphics and Printing Ltd., China

5 7 9 10 8 6 4

introduction

In the days before digital photography, life seemed simple: Film was processed into either prints or transparencies, and for the well organized, prints were stored in albums and transparencies viewed via slide projector. For many, however, the task was onerous and the shoe box was where the photographic collection ended up. The advent of digital photography has been liberating. Every week millions of digital images are created, some to be printed and displayed; most however, are lost in the digital equivalent of that shoe box. Now help is at hand. *How to Do Just about Anything with Your Digital Photos* is packed full of suggestions on how to organize, present, and share your digital photographs.

Creating your own family tree, a poster of a day trip, fun borders, or personalized cards are all easy projects to create—just follow the simple step-by-step instructions.

What you'll learn

For many, digital camera technology is rife with baffling technology that is hard to fathom. Section 1—*Hardware and Software*—converts the jargon into plain language. Here we offer advice on what to look for in cameras, scanners, computers, printers, and software— from how many megapixels you need, through what computing power is required, to what software applications are appropriate.

In section 2—*Getting Started*— you'll learn not only how to transfer photos from your camera (or scanner) to your computer, but also how to organize your picture files and copy ("burn") them onto a CD or DVD.

Before you get to the projects themselves, in section 3—*Image Editing and Printing*—we'll show you how applications like Adobe's Photoshop Elements have made photo retouching and enhancement available to the amateur at the click of a button. You'll learn about the basic menus and tools used in image editing and how they can be used to correct exposure or color, crop or resize images, even how to sharpen "soft"-looking images or get rid of that annoying red-eye problem. This section also explains about "layers." Learning how to use layers is an essential part of image editing, and almost all the projects contained in this book involve the use of layers. You'll be amazed at how easy they are to master. Finally, section 3 finishes with information on printing. Even inexpensive inkjet printers offer exceptional print quality, and most will accept the various media we've used in the creation of the projects. However, it's important to know what the best settings are to avoid disappointing results. We also provide information on getting your images printed professionally if there's something you can't do at home, such as making poster-size prints or printing on a media that your home printer can't cope with.

The projects

We begin the projects in section 4—*Print Projects*—where you'll receive step-by-step instructions on creating a variety of fun and practical ideas, ranging from a personalized birthday invitation and a vacation album to creating your own personal stationery. Each project is devised to present your digital photographs in a different way.

Section 5—*Special Print Projects*—shows you how to use your digital photos in new and exciting ways. In this section we'll explain how to make your

own sticky labels, how to print onto T-shirts, even how to produce your own refrigerator magnets.

In section 6—*Screen Projects*—we concentrate on how the Internet can help you to share your photos with family and friends. The Web has enabled the sharing of digital photographs to flourish. Nowadays most people have an Internet connection and use e-mail, and in this section we cut through the "webspeak" jargon to show you just how easy it is to get your photographs "online." There are two main options available: to create projects on your home computer and then transfer them to a Web space that nearly all Internet service providers (ISPs) provide, or to

use an online service to assemble the images into a photo gallery, slide show, or even a website—*How to Do Just about Anything with Your Digital Photos* includes creative and achievable projects for both options.

Finally section 7—*Reference*—is packed with helpful advice, Web addresses, and details of the website (*see page 166*) that accompanies this book, and which is available to all purchasers of *How to Do Just about Anything with Your Digital Photos*. Log on to this site and you'll be able to download the borders and templates used in the creation of some of the projects, along with helpful links to other relevant online resources.

Earlier sections of How to Do Just about Anything with Your Digital Photos *provide succinct but invaluable advice on how to enhance your photos—and there's even information on how to prepare your images for the Web.*

hardware and software

The explosion of interest in digital photography in recent times has brought about a vast number of new products and manufacturers—not just in terms of cameras, which have seen electronics companies competing with traditional camera manufacturers—but also in terms of digital-imaging software, printers, scanners, and many other accessories. But before you buy any photographic or computer equipment, it is a good idea to do some research. If you are reasonably experienced and know what you want, this is simply a case of getting the best deal. If you are less sure, this chapter provides some ground rules for you to follow. Although we cannot recommend specific products or brands, we can give you the names of several organizations that offer impartial advice and product reviews in this constantly changing marketplace. Contact details for these can be found on page 166.

IN THIS CHAPTER . . .

"capturing" your photos

The projects contained in this book rely on your being able to "capture" photographs digitally—that is, you need to be able to create digital picture files that can be stored on a computer. There are two ways to do this. One is to buy a digital camera and take your photos, then transfer the picture files to the computer. Another is to scan existing photographs using a scanner, which converts your photos into a digital file. This file can then be placed on the computer. Here we offer some basic advice on cameras and scanners.

This Fuji FinePix S5000 is a 3MP camera designed to look and feel like a single lens reflex camera.

COMPARATIVE IMAGE SIZE VS MEGAPIXELS (MP)

An image from a 3MP camera printed at 300 dpi on a letter-size piece of paper

An image from a 4MP camera printed at 300 dpi on a letter-size piece of paper

An image from a 6MP camera printed at 300 dpi on a letter-size piece of paper

Choosing a digital camera

When deciding which camera to buy, one of the key things to look for is the number of megapixels (MP) the camera has. All digital images are made up of individual picture elements ("pixels"). The higher the number of pixels, the better the image quality. Today, megapixel values range from 1MP to 8MP. As a general rule of thumb, 1MP is sufficient only if your images will be viewed on a computer. If you want to make photo-quality prints, then you really need a camera with a minimum of 3MP. The chart on the left shows the relative size of photo-quality prints that can be obtained with varying megapixel counts.

The back of a typical compact digital camera, showing various menu and control buttons.

Of course, image quality is also governed by the quality of the lens. Fortunately, the lenses found in modern compact cameras all tend to be of good quality, but if in doubt you can check the lens accuracy of most camera models on www.dpreview.com.

Another key consideration is the power of the optical zoom. Most compact cameras have a 3X or 4X zoom, which is adequate for most situations. Ignore any reference to digital zoom, as this feature can produce poor quality images.

Memory cards and card readers
Your camera will come with a memory card on which to store the images. However, this will have a relatively small capacity, and you won't be able to store many images on it. You will want to buy a second card with a much larger capacity (see the chart, right, for guidance).

Images are usually transferred from the camera to the computer via

There are a variety of memory storage cards and card readers. The greater the capacity of the memory card, the more images you can fit on it. Make sure you know which cards your camera takes–it could support a number of options.

✎ getting technical

Images stored on a memory card
Cameras vary in the range of quality options they offer. This chart is based on a typical mid-range 2.1 megapixel camera.

Memory capacity (MB)	Low-quality images (64KB)	High-quality images (500KB)
16	250	32
32	500	64
64	1,000	128
256	4,000	512
512	8,000	1,024

a special cable called a USB cable. Read the camera's manual carefully for full directions. An alternative method is to connect a card reader to the computer. To transfer your images, simply remove the memory card from the camera, and insert the card into the card reader. This will launch software on the computer that will show you how to copy the images from the card across to the hard disk on the computer.

There are a wide variety of memory card formats available. These are not usually interchangeable, so if you buy a card reader, make sure that it is compatible with the memory card that fits your camera.

Scanners
If you intend to scan [create a digital image from a real photo] photographs, a mid-range or even a budget flatbed scanner will suffice–but be sure to check whether it has a minimum resolution of 1,200 dpi (dots per inch). Ignore any figures quoting interpolated resolution. Interpolated resolution is what the scanner will guess at instead of actually scan.

If you want to scan transparencies or color negatives from which prints have been made, there are two options: a slide converter that fits over the lid of a flatbed scanner, or a dedicated film scanner. Again, if you buy a film scanner, ensure the resolution is no less than 1,200 dpi.

Another important consideration is "bit depth" (the amount of color information a scanner can interpret). For flatbed scanners, 24-bit is sufficient, but 36-bit is preferable for scanning film.

An example of a mid-range flatbed scanner, used for scanning color photographs.

computers and printers

Having the right computer and printer enables you to undertake a variety of projects, from making a scrapbook to creating an online gallery. If you bought your computer no earlier than 2003, it is probably more than adequate for the projects shown in this book. If it's any older, use the checklist below to see how your model compares. You'll also want top-quality photo prints from your printer, so here we offer some basic advice.

Today's PCs will have more than enough processing power for your digital photo needs.

🖱 know your equipment

NEW COMPUTERS
Essential features

✔ USB2 or Firewire2 port (socket)—Both are backwardly compatible with USB(1) and Firewire(1) respectively. These offer the fastest connection from your camera, card reader, or scanner to the computer.

✔ CD-R—52x24x52x are the speeds for writing a CD-R, or a CD-RW, or reading an existing CD. A fast CD writer is well worth the little extra cost.

✔ DVD-R—4x4x are the speeds for writing a DVD-R or a DVD-RW. For the presentation of still images, the cheaper CD-R will suffice. DVD-R is really necessary only if you intend to create home movies. A fast DVD writer will sell at a premium, as the technology is newer than CD-R.

🖱 know your equipment

OLDER COMPUTERS
Specification checklist

✔ Does it have a USB connection?

✔ Does it have a minimum of 128MB of RAM?

✔ Does it have a hard disk in excess of 40MB?

✔ Does it have a CD-R to write (burn) CDs?

Computers
If your existing computer does not have the specifications outlined on the chart (left), you should consider replacing it. The choice, then, becomes choosing between a Windows PC and an Apple Macintosh. Both PC and Macintosh computers are easy to use, but the advantage with PCs is that they are considerably cheaper. Even an entry-level computer these days has phenomenal processing power. Unless you hope to graduate into professional digital photography, a PC should meet all your needs.

If you do decide to buy a brand new computer, make sure that it has all the features outlined on the new computer checklist (*see page 12*).

An additional benefit of buying a new computer is that it will have the latest operating system, which is likely to offer you new features and increased functionality as well as being easier to use.

Most new desktop computers come with either a 17-in. conventional monitor or a 15-in. flat screen. Both types normally display a resolution of 1,024 pixels wide by 768 pixels deep. Portable notebook computers are popular, but they usually come with smaller screens with lower resolution. Also, portables are usually more expensive.

Printers

The quality achieved by modern color printers just keeps on getting better and better. Many can now match the best photographic printing from film.

There are two main technologies: inkjet and laser. The inkjet is by far the most popular with home users because of its low purchase cost. Color laser printers used to be very expensive, but prices continue to fall and may soon reach the level of the inkjet.

The running costs of inkjets are high, however. Most ink cartridges are expensive, and special paper must be used to obtain top-quality printing. Color laser cartridges are not cheap, but they last much longer than inkjet cartridges. Color laser printers are also more tolerant of poorer-quality paper.

getting technical

How many colors?

Many inkjet printers and some color laser printers use six or even seven colors to print an image. The quality is better than printers that use just four colors, particularly when printing photographs, but replacing ink cartridges is more expensive.

Most printers are limited to using only letter, 8.5 x 11-in. (A4) paper, although tabloid, 11 x 17-in. (A3) prints are possible on some inkjets. Many inkjets boast a resolution of at least 1,440 dpi. Lasers are normally lower, at 600 dpi. However, these figures are not directly comparable because each technology distributes the dots in a different way.

Another important consideration is the range and weight (thickness) of paper or other media used in the printer. A list of the media used in this book can be found on page 44.

see page 12, page 44

jargon buster

- **USB** is a port (or cable) for connecting your digital camera and/or card reader.

- **RAM** is the "working space" made available by the computer to run the various applications. An item is memorized in RAM only for as long as the computer remains switched on.

- **The hard disk** is where all the files on your computer are stored. Unlike with RAM, the files will still be stored on the hard disk when you turn the computer on again.

- **CD and DVD** can read only existing CDs or DVDs.

- **CD-R (write once)** and **CD-RW (rewrite again and again)** are fitted to nearly all new computers, with DVD-R (write once) and DVD-RW (rewrite again and again) as an option.

Modern inkjet printers can produce photo-quality prints in a variety of sizes, and most are able to make borderless prints, as shown here.

13

image-editing software

To present your digital photos, you will need image-editing software. This is often bundled with your digital camera or scanner. Adobe Photoshop Elements is particularly popular. It is inexpensive and was developed specifically with the amateur photographer in mind. There are many other software programs available to enhance, present, and share your photographs, as a glance at any computer or digital photography magazine will reveal. Fortunately, most image-editing software uses a similar interface and set of tools. A variety of popular software application interfaces are shown opposite.

Selected from the Enhance menu, the Quick Fix palette enables image improvements to be made with both the Before and After views visible.

SHORTCUT BAR

MAIN WINDOW

IMAGE WINDOW

TOOLS PALETTE

IMAGE % ZOOM

IMAGE SIZE

RECIPES PALETTE

LAYERS PALETTE

HINTS PALETTE

PALETTE DOCK

Photoshop Elements is typical of many image-editing applications. It features "recipes" that help you perform tasks such as "Remove scratches and specks."

There are a great many image-editing programs available. Often when you buy a new camera, scanner, or printer, you will be given free software.

For the projects in this book, we used Adobe Photoshop Elements, Microsoft MS Plus! Digital Media Edition, and MS Moviemaker on a PC. Elements is available for both PC and Apple Macintosh. iPhoto and iMovie are options for the Mac.

File formats

In order to open a file in a particular software program, the file has to be recognized by that program. On a PC, the file is identified by its three-character file extension (the three letters after the full stop). For example, Photoshop Elements files have the file extension .psd. The file myphoto.psd therefore can be opened in Photoshop Elements. Macs are different: the file extension is not necessary for the software to recognize the file.

All image-editing applications have their own proprietary file formats, so it is not usually possible to open them in another program. However, generic formats such as JPEGs and TIFFs can be opened in different applications. JPEG (.jpg on the PC) is the most common format. This is the format that nearly all digital cameras use to store the photographs that you shoot. On some high-end cameras, there is an option to use RAW format. It is called RAW because the data that makes up the image is untouched by the camera's built-in processing software.

For the purposes of this book, however, we will assume that the photos in your digital camera are JPEG. With JPEG, the image data are "compressed" so that more images can fit on the memory card. With highly compressed images, there is a trade-off with quality. Most digital cameras offer some control over the amount of compression. "Good," "Better," or "Best" are typical options, with "Good" being the smallest files and "Best," the largest.

getting started

Before you can show off your digital photographs to your family and friends, you first have to transfer images from your camera or scanner into the computer. If you are working on a PC, your computer will have numerous "wizards" (help boxes) to show you how to do this. Apple Macintosh computers also have a number of tip boxes to make your life easier. And before your photo collection becomes too large, it is prudent to plan how you are going to organize it. Once you have organized your files, you'd be wise to archive them onto a CD. Finally, to get perfect prints, you'll need to spend time setting up your printer correctly and choosing the appropriate paper. This chapter will help you achieve all those things and more.

IN THIS CHAPTER . . .

getting an image from a digital camera

The first stage of accessing the photographs you've taken with your digital camera is to connect your camera to the computer. Once you've done that, you can start to copy your images.

There are three ways to connect to your computer:

❶ connect the camera direct to your computer via USB or Firewire

❷ insert the memory card into a card reader, which is already connected to the computer,

❸ place the camera into a docking station and connect the station to the computer.

To connect, plug one end of the cable into the camera, card reader, or docking station USB port and the other end into the computer USB (for some models, Firewire may be an alternative to USB).

You will probably be prompted to install software that comes with the camera, card reader, or docking station before you connect the cable. Once this is complete, an icon should appear on the desktop containing all the photos stored in the camera's memory card.

→ tip

Connect mode

With some models, the camera should not be left on *Picture Taking* or *Reviewing* mode, or it will not connect to the computer. If this is the case with your model, ensure that the camera is set to *Connect* mode. Not all cameras use the same terminology, but it should be obvious from the options on your camera's controls which this is.

CONNECTING VIA USB CABLE

Most digital cameras connect to a computer using a USB port, although some use a specialist Firewire connector. The camera has to be turned on, so be aware that the battery will be running down while you transfer images.

CONNECTING VIA A CARD READER

This single-format card reader accepts a 1GB compact flash card with enough space for 3000 medium-resolution images.

Double-click the card reader icon on the desktop. This fires up a screen showing thumbnails of the images on the card. They can then be transferred in the way previously described. If you right-click a thumbnail photo in Windows XP, you can view a large preview image.

CONNECTING VIA A DOCKING STATION

The camera docking/transfer process will vary with manufacturer. The Kodak EasyShare range is typical. The camera is placed into the dock, which is connected by cable to the computer. Pushing the connect button will automatically transfer the images to the computer.

Docking stations (or cradles) enable you to transfer images directly to your computer while charging the camera's battery at the same time.

TRANSFERRING IMAGES TO YOUR COMPUTER

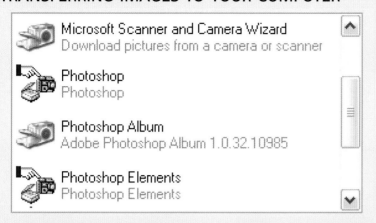

◀ On a Windows XP computer, connecting the camera by cable to the computer brings up the option *Select the program to launch this action*. This lists the applications that are able to import photos directly from the camera, among them the *Microsoft Scanner and Camera Wizard*.

▲ After the welcome screen, you will be prompted both to select the photos that you want to transfer and to choose their location on your computer. At the end of the process, you have the option of publishing the images to a website if you have already registered with a suitable service, such as MSN Groups *(see pages 158–159).*

continued ▶▶

GETTING IMAGES USING AN APPLICATION

getting technical

GO WIRELESS

Some computers and cameras feature technology that utilizes radio waves to transfer information. If you use such a "Wireless-enabled" computer and camera, it is possible to transfer photos without any physical connection between the two. The technology is similar to a mobile phone. Many notebook computers have this WI-FI facility, and desktop computers are catching up quickly. Before purchasing a digital camera, check that it is WI-FI enabled if you wish to transfer images this way.

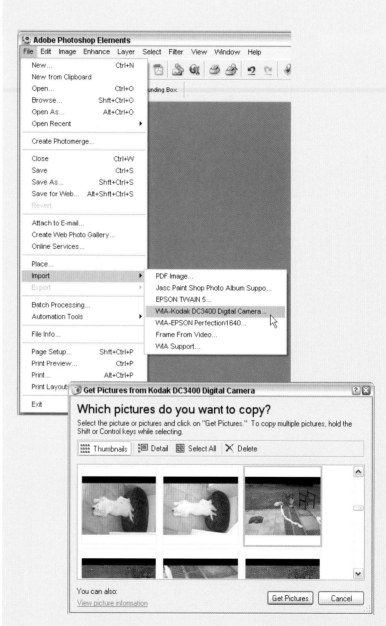

▲ You can also transfer images through applications such as Photoshop Elements. Once you have launched the application, select the camera using the *Import* option from the *File* menu. You will be prompted to select the photos that you wish to copy. These will then be opened in Photoshop Elements.

GETTING IMAGES WITH
THE CAMERA ICON

▲ Clicking the camera icon prompts a window offering various options. *Get pictures from camera* and *Delete all pictures on camera* are self-explanatory. Clicking *Show camera properties* reveals the number of photos taken and the number remaining, along with the current picture-size setting in pixels.

◀ The *View* menu gives the option of seeing the images as a filmstrip. If you cannot see the filmstrip, right-click the folder to view its properties and select *What kind of folder do you want?* from the *Customize* tab. Then make sure that either *Pictures* or *Photo Album* is selected.

scanning and transferring photos

To convert a real photograph into pixels on your screen, or "scan" a picture, you first need to install scanner software and then connect a scanner to either a USB or Firewire port. Scanner software comprises two parts: The first part may include options to print the scanned image directly, or to fax or e-mail it. The second part (known as TWAIN) enables you to scan from within any application (such as Photoshop Elements) that supports TWAIN. For example, if you are using a word-processing package, you may want to scan in a document for a report.

HOW TO SCAN AN IMAGE USING PHOTOSHOP ELEMENTS

① From the Photoshop Elements *File* menu, select *Import/TWAIN* option. A typical scanner has two options: full auto or manual scan. If the manual option (above) looks too intimidating, use the *auto* option.

② Whichever method you use, the resulting scan will appear within Elements. You can then use options such as *Resize and Rotate* to alter, enhance, and retouch the image.

TRANSFERRING USING THE
SCANNER AND CAMERA WIZARD

1 Scanning an old black-and-white photo as a color picture results in a richer image. Click the preview button to see the photo in its prescanned state.

2 If you click on *Next*, a window appears prompting a name and place to store your pictures. By default, this will be the *My Pictures* folder, although you can select an alternative location and folder if you wish. You will then have to select a file format (*see box below*) for the scanned photo. The default option is JPEG (.jpg). Clicking *Next* again starts the scanning process.

3 When the scan is finished, you can view the photo and rotate it if necessary. Here, *View as Filmstrip* has been selected from the *View* menu. This is useful if you have scanned a number of images and wish to select one to view at a larger scale.

---

getting technical

Saving photos

If you scan an image using the *Scanner and Camera Wizard*, you will be asked to select a file format (*see pages 14–15*). The choices are all generic. For example .BMP, .JPG, .TIF, and .PNG are used by most Windows applications. If you scan using TWAIN, the image will be saved in the application's own file format. Photoshop Elements uses the format .PSD. This format has various advantages. As a PSD-formatted file, an image can have a number of layers (*see pages 38–39*) so several images can be combined—essential for most of the projects shown in this book. The transparency (*Opacity*) of each layer can be varied, so, for example, an image on a layer above can be translucent rather than opaque, partially revealing the image on the layer below. Once you are happy with the scan, save it. If you want to share the image, use *Save As* to save a copy of it in a generic format such as .JPG.

organizing image files and burning CDs/DVDs

Keeping track of files on your computer has always been a challenge, and now when you start adding large numbers of photos from your digital camera, the problem is compounded—particularly when you consider a typical file name is DCP_2646.JPG. So what's the best system to use? Below we tell you how to get started.

Problems can arise as soon as the photo is taken. For example, on a typical vacation, is it possible to remember every place name where a photo was taken, or the names of the people you met? Help is at hand in the form of a feature of the JPEG format that most digital cameras use. It is called EXIF (Exchangeable Image File Format).

EXIF includes technical data like exposure and shutter speed but it also includes date and time information which can be recorded for every photo that you take. If you want to be really well organised, you might want to keep a notebook to mark down the time for each different group of photos you take.

This might help remember which order your shots are taken when out and about on holiday, but how do you organize your photos once back home?

In Windows XP, the folder *My Documents/My Pictures* is the default storage area for photos. You can, of course, choose a different location. It can be time-consuming to rename every file using a description rather than the numerical file name generated by the camera, but in the long run this may be time-saving when it comes to retrieving a specific image.

A better option is to create folders with descriptive names and use the folder's thumbnail view to select the appropriate images to put in it. Avoid putting too many folders within folders.

→ tip

File info in elements
If you open a file in Elements and then select *File Info* from the *File* menu, clicking the *EXIF* tab will reveal a lot of information about that image, including the camera used and the time and date that the photo was taken. Under the *General* tab, you can add more information to the image, such as a caption.

Making CDs and DVDs
Both Windows XP and the Macintosh OS allow for drag-and-drop CD writing, with no additional software needed. CD writers are usually supplied with additional software that gives access to additional features. Either Nero Burning Rom or Easy CD Creator are supplied with most Windows XP machines. Toast is the preferred option on the Mac.

The importance of organizing your photographs becomes even more apparent when you make CDs or DVDs. It can be irritating to look at a CD made six months earlier and find photos labeled only with numerical file names, providing no means of finding an image.

Using simple notes like those taken at "Gail's Graduation" enables you to organize photos on your computer. The shots taken between 16:57 and 17:00 are of the graduation ceremony, so files between these times can be put in a separate folder. Adding a numeral at the beginning of the folder name ensures that the folders appear in the correct sequence. Otherwise they default to alphabetical order.

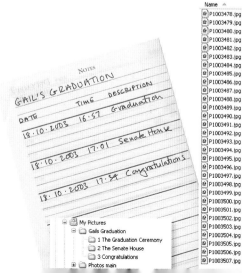

Name	Size	Type	Date Created
P1003478.jpg	288 KB	Generic JPEG	18/10/2003 17:34
P1003479.jpg	160 KB	Generic JPEG	18/10/2003 17:34
P1003480.jpg	288 KB	Generic JPEG	18/10/2003 17:34
P1003481.jpg	224 KB	Generic JPEG	18/10/2003 17:35
P1003482.jpg	192 KB	Generic JPEG	18/10/2003 17:35
P1003483.jpg	224 KB	Generic JPEG	18/10/2003 17:36
P1003484.jpg	128 KB	Generic JPEG	18/10/2003 17:36
P1003485.jpg	320 KB	Generic JPEG	18/10/2003 17:36
P1003486.jpg	352 KB	Generic JPEG	18/10/2003 17:36
P1003487.jpg	352 KB	Generic JPEG	18/10/2003 17:37
P1003488.jpg	384 KB	Generic JPEG	18/10/2003 17:37
P1003489.jpg	320 KB	Generic JPEG	18/10/2003 17:38
P1003490.jpg	224 KB	Generic JPEG	18/10/2003 18:35
P1003491.jpg	384 KB	Generic JPEG	18/10/2003 18:36
P1003492.jpg	384 KB	Generic JPEG	18/10/2003 18:36
P1003493.jpg	320 KB	Generic JPEG	18/10/2003 18:36
P1003494.jpg	352 KB	Generic JPEG	18/10/2003 18:36
P1003495.jpg	320 KB	Generic JPEG	18/10/2003 18:37
P1003496.jpg	192 KB	Generic JPEG	18/10/2003 19:26
P1003497.jpg	224 KB	Generic JPEG	18/10/2003 19:27
P1003498.jpg	64 KB	Generic JPEG	18/10/2003 19:27
P1003499.jpg	256 KB	Generic JPEG	18/10/2003 19:27
P1003500.jpg	256 KB	Generic JPEG	18/10/2003 19:28
P1003501.jpg	352 KB	Generic JPEG	18/10/2003 19:28
P1003502.jpg	96 KB	Generic JPEG	18/10/2003 19:28
P1003503.jpg	160 KB	Generic JPEG	18/10/2003 19:28
P1003504.jpg	224 KB	Generic JPEG	18/10/2003 19:29
P1003505.jpg	288 KB	Generic JPEG	18/10/2003 19:29
P1003506.jpg	320 KB	Generic JPEG	18/10/2003 19:30
P1003507.jpg	352 KB	Generic JPEG	18/10/2003 19:30

BURNING A CD

▲ Copying files onto a CD is very simple. With a blank CD in the CD writer, double-click the *CD-RW Drive* (see next dialog box) in *My Computer*. Drag the folders to be copied and drop them onto the blank window. Select *Write these files to CD* from the *CD Writing Tasks* panel, and the job is done. If you change your mind, use *Delete temporary files* to remove them. You can toggle between *Task* and *Explore* mode by clicking the *Folders* button. Toggling is useful if you are copying a lot of folders or if you are not sure in which folder photos you wish to copy have been stored.

▲ If you plan to send your CD to a family member or friend and do not know what type of computer or operating system (OS) they use, it is generally safer to use a popular application like Nero Express. This handy program has a wider range of format options than Window XP's own CD burner. You can even make a video CD that can be played on a TV-based DVD player.

▲ If you want to create a DVD rather than a CD, you will need a dedicated application like Adobe Encore. If you're working on a Macintosh, you can use iDVD. The 4.7Gb capacity of a DVD makes it much more suited to recording video rather than still images.

image editing and printing

Although digital cameras generally take great pictures, there will inevitably be occasions when a photo needs some improvement. You turned off the red-eye option by mistake, your subject is in shadow, or your camera angle was skewed—these are all common mistakes. If you are scanning old color photos, they may be faded or have an unwanted color bias that you want to correct. In this chapter we show you how to fix those mistakes or enhance old photos. Our demonstrations use Adobe Photoshop Elements extensively, since this is currently the most popular image-editing software for amateur photographers. You might not use this program, but don't worry because Photoshop Elements shares many of its features with other popular image-editing programs.

IN THIS CHAPTER . . .

image-editing tools

Opening an image-editing application for the first time can seem daunting. Fortunately, Adobe Photoshop Elements has been devised with the amateur photographer and computer novice in mind. Over the next few pages, we explain how to use the basic image-editing tools.

The *Toolbox* is a good place to start. It contains the tools that you will use to select a particular area of an image in order to work on it—a simple rectangle, perhaps, or an irregular shape like the outline of a building. There are brushes and pencils to draw with and an eraser to remove anything no longer needed. There are simple retouching tools to blur or sharpen, and others to clone an area so that it can be applied elsewhere. This is very useful if you need to "patch up" a damaged photo or if you want to remove unwanted objects from an image, such as a garden tool from an otherwise pristine lawn. The *Eyedropper* enables you to sample any color in an image. This is useful if, for example, you want to match a border color to one in the image. There is a *Text* tool, a *Zoom* tool, and the *Foreground* and *Background color selectors*. You will soon become familiar with the tools you use most often.

For every tool there is a *Hints* palette that helps you to complete a task, along with the *How To/Recipes* palette that actually does the job for you—for example, *Fix a torn photo*. In the *Palette Well,* the tabbed palettes offer more features and effects. The *Undo History* palette, for instance, shows recently completed tasks. Each can be undone by moving the arrow to a previous stage.

The Toolbox *holds 24 tools for creating and editing images. Some have flyout menus that offer variations of the basic tool. All tools have additional options, like size or color. These are available from the* Options *bar.*

RECTANGULAR MARQUEE TOOL
Selects a rectangular area on your image so you can work on that particular part of it (this is referred to as a "selection") without affecting the rest of the image.
FLYOUT: **Elliptical Marquee.**

MOVE TOOL
Enables you to drag a selected area to a new position.

LASSO TOOL
Draws a freehand selection around an image.
FLYOUT: **Polygonal and Magnetic Lasso tool.**

MAGIC WAND TOOL
Makes a selection based on common colors. Click on the blue in a sky, for example, and the clouds will be excluded from the selection. The Tolerance setting in the Options bar controls how far the selection extends into adjacent colors.

SELECTION BRUSH TOOL
Enables an area of the image to be selected by painting it. Use this tool when a soft edge is required.

CROP TOOL
Makes a selection of a smaller area within an image and then crops the image to that area.

RECTANGLE TOOL
Draws a rectangle filled with the foreground color.
FLYOUT: **Rounded Rectangle, Ellipse, Polygon, Line, Custom Shape, Shape selection.**

HORIZONTAL TYPE TOOL
Enters normal horizontal type on a new layer. Set other font attributes with the Options bar.
FLYOUT: **Vertical Type, Horizontal Type Mask, Vertical Type Mask.**

PAINT BUCKET TOOL
Fills a selection with a color or pattern.

GRADIENT TOOL
Fills a selection with graduated rather than flat colors. Select the style of gradient and the colors from the Options *bar.*

BRUSH TOOL
Paints brushstrokes. Select brush styles and sizes from the Options *bar.*
FLYOUT: **Impressionist.**

PENCIL TOOL
Draws hard-edge lines. Select brush styles and sizes from the Options *bar.*

ERASER TOOL
Erases as it is dragged across an image.
FLYOUT: **Background Eraser, Magic Eraser.**

RED-EYE BRUSH TOOL
Removes red-eye effect on photos taken with a flash.

BLUR TOOL
Blurs hard edges as it is dragged across an image.

SHARPEN TOOL
Sharpens soft edges as it is dragged across an image.

SPONGE TOOL
Changes the color saturation as it is dragged across an image.

SMUDGE TOOL
Smudges colors as it is dragged across an image.

DODGE TOOL
Lightens an area as it is dragged across an image.

BURN TOOL
Darkens an area as it is dragged across an image.

CLONE STAMP TOOL
Copies an area of an image so that it can be "dropped" in a new location. The size of the area to be cloned is determined by the brush or pen sizes, which are selected from the Options *bar.*
FLYOUT: **Pattern Stamp tool.**

EYEDROPPER TOOL
Samples colors within an image. When clicked, the sample color becomes the new foreground color.

HAND TOOL
Drag over an image to view areas not visible.

ZOOM TOOL
Zooms in or out of an image. The actual image size remains unchanged.

FOREGROUND and BACKGROUND COLOR SELECTORS
Selects the foreground or background color.

If there is a small arrow at the bottom right of the tool icon, holding the icon down brings up the flyout menu with variations of the tool.

When a tool is selected, its options automatically appear in the Options *bar. The* Brush *tool options comprise type and size along with a drop-down menu showing* Presets, Mode, *and* Opacity.

The Palette Well *contains tabbed palettes. These snap back automatically after use. If you want them to stay open permanently, they can be dragged out of the* Well *and moved elsewhere in the work area. Here, the* Layers *palette has been dragged out.*

basic image-editing techniques

Before you can undertake any task in Elements (or in any other software), you have to make a selection. If you want to make a change to the entire image—like rotate or flip—it can be selected from the *Image* drop-down menu. If you want to change just part of the image, you have to select that section. Once selected, that part of the image can be worked on without affecting the rest of the picture.

A photograph that has been transferred from your digital camera will almost always be in generic JPEG (.JPG) format (*see page 15*) unless it has been set up otherwise.

When you open a photo in Elements, the image will appear as a locked background. This means it cannot be edited. Before you can apply a transformation, such as *Rotation*, the

background needs to be converted to an editable layer. Duplicate the layer (*see box*) to save damaging the original photograph. If you resize a photograph, bear in mind that quality is likely to suffer if you enlarge it more than about 10%. If you require larger images on a regular basis, it is better to increase the quality and resolution setting in your camera. Reducing image size is not a problem.

→ **tip**

Duplicate Layer

Before making changes to an image, you can, of course, make a copy and work on that. If you want to be able to compare the original with the altered version, you can duplicate the layer (*see pages 38–39*). This makes it easier to compare the two versions. In the *Layers* palette, click on the original layer and drag-and-drop it over the *Create New Layer* icon. A duplicate will be created. When you save a layered file, it will be in Elements' own .PSD file format, not a JPEG.

RESIZING

▲ Select *Resize/Image Size* from the *Image* drop-down menu. To change the image size, type in a new *Width* or *Height*. Keeping *Constrain Proportions* checked ensures the image retains the same proportions as before. *Resample Image* should be checked.

▲ If you want to create a border around the image, change *Canvas Size* rather than *Image Size*. If the *Anchor Point* is central, the additional space will be added equally on all sides.

▲ The *Image* drop-down menu contains a range of transformations that can be applied to the entire image.

CROPPING

▲ You can set the crop size (here, 6 x 6 in./15 x 15 cm.) in the *Options* menu, having first selected the *Crop* tool. Drag the marquee to the area required. The image will be cropped to this size. Use the right mouse button to cancel if required.

ROTATING

Resize

Rotate

▲ Use the *Elliptical Marquee* to draw a selection; holding the Shift key down constrains the shape to a circle. Clicking the *Move* tool will make handles appear around the selection. Drag one of the corner handles to rotate the selection to a new position.

MAKING SELECTIONS

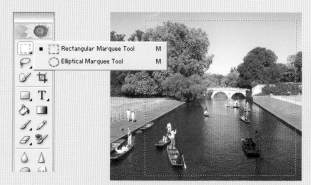

▲ Use one of the *Marquee* tools (here, the *Rectangular Marquee*) and press the Shift and Alt keys. Place the cursor in the middle of the image and drag it toward the edge. The selection will be centered around the original cursor position.

▲ The *Magnetic Lasso* tool is another useful selection tool. It gets its name from the fact that as you run the cursor along the object you're selecting, the selection line "sticks" to the object. It does this by differentiating between pixel colors.

▲ Using the *Magic Wand* tool with the *Tolerance* set to 20 in the *Options* menu, click in the central sky area. The resulting selection will contain only a small area of sky.

▲ If you increase the *Tolerance* setting to 100, all of the sky is selected. The enlarged detail shows that some of the trees are also included in the selection. This method works best when there is a big color difference between areas.

correcting exposure

Most digital cameras take good-quality photos most of the time. However, if you leave your camera on fully automatic mode, or if your camera doesn't have any manual override, there will be times when the camera doesn't make the best decision.

This is particularly true of scenes that are partly in shadow. To retain detail within the shadow would mean lightening the rest of the image to an unacceptable degree, so the camera makes a compromise. Elements has a number of tools to overcome exposure problems. There will be occasions when you want to use these tools to create a special effect, like increasing contrast.

Sometimes you need to mask a photo to apply the improvement to a particular area. Use one of the selection methods described on pages 28-29 and always apply the correction to a duplicate of the original photo layer.

Since every image is different, Elements offers alternative methods for achieving a given result. With a little trial and error, most exposure problems can be overcome. As your confidence builds, you may find using more than one technique on a single image will yield the best results.

QUICK FIX EXPOSURE CORRECTION

▲ An alternative method of improving this photo is to use *Quick Fix* from the *Enhance* drop-down menu. With the *Fill Flash* option selected, drag the slider to +31. The shadow area is opened up considerably.

SELECTIVE EXPOSURE CORRECTION

Applying an overall correction will not always work. Here there is a large shadow area in the background and a brightly lit wall in the foreground, which must be excluded from the lightening process. On a duplicate layer, use *Fill Flash*. Drag the Lighter slider to +19. This opens up the whole image.

Zoom the image to a convenient size. Using the *Polygonal Lasso* tool in a series of tiny steps, trace around the foreground area. Make sure the end of the trace joins with the beginning. Now delete this area to enable the original image to show through in this area. Use the Ctrl+X shortcut to delete.

The original photo and the original photo with *Fill Flash* applied overall.

The *Fill Flash* Layer with the foreground removed to let the original photo show through.

correcting color

Digital cameras are very good at recording color, so it is unlikely that your photos will need much improvement in this area. It is more likely that you'll want to change a color for effect rather than to correct. This is not the case with scanned color photos, however, especially old ones where colors may have faded inconsistently.

QUICK FIX COLOR CORRECTION

▲ The *Quick Fix* color correction method works in the same way as using *Quick Fix* to adjust exposure (*see page 32*). Select *Quick Fix* from the *Enhance* drop-down menu and then click on the *Color Correction* button. You'll be given two options. One is *Auto Color*, which, if selected, assesses the image and makes what the computer thinks are the appropriate changes. The other is *Hue/Saturation*, which enables you to manually alter the hue, saturation, and lightness of the image. In both cases, the *After* image previews the effect of the correction on your original image. As soon as you are happy with the correction, click *OK*.

ENHANCE COLOR CORRECTION

▲ There are five color correction options available from the *Enhance* drop-down menu: *Quick Fix>Color Correction*; *Auto Color Correction*; *Adjust Color>Color Cast*; *Adjust Color >Hue/Saturation*; and *Adjust Color >Replace Color*. In this shot the color is attractive but looks a bit unnatural.

▲ Click *Auto Color Correction,* and Elements will fix the color for you. The snow is now bluer and more natural looking, but the picture looks a little dirty.

SELECTIVE COLOR CORRECTION

▲ The two previous methods apply an overall color change. *Replace Color* offers you more discrimination. This method also uses the *Eyedropper* tool to sample a color to be replaced. This time the area just in front of the tobogganer is selected as representative of the general snow color. Drag the *Hue* slider to the left until the sample shows it as blue. The *Fuzziness* slider controls the area of the image to which the new color will be applied. The result is a bluer snow, but with some warm, sunny highlights—much more atmospheric.

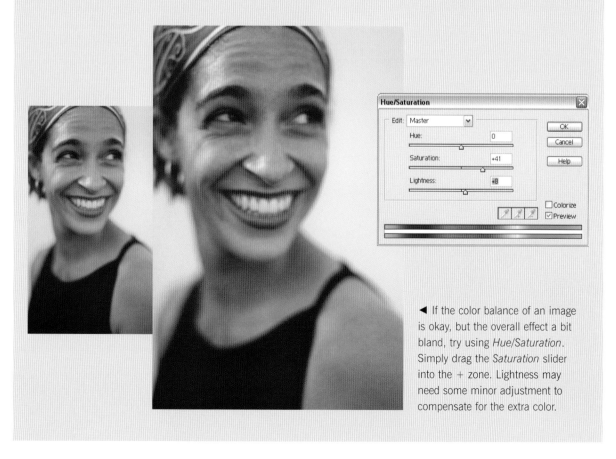

◄ If the color balance of an image is okay, but the overall effect a bit bland, try using *Hue/Saturation*. Simply drag the *Saturation* slider into the + zone. Lightness may need some minor adjustment to compensate for the extra color.

sharpening images and fixing red-eye

You may find that the photos you take with your digital camera look a little "soft"—that is, not out of focus—but just a bit blurred. Photoshop Elements has an excellent tool that helps you "sharpen" your images. Another problem is red-eye. Red-eye occurs when the red blood vessels in a subject's eyes have been lit by the camera's flash. You can fix that, too.

Even the most experienced photographers sometimes find that an image looks a little soft, or fuzzy. There are several reasons for not having razor-sharp images every time. For example, the photo may have been taken in poor light or the camera's autofocus didn't deliver the intended effect. A scanned color print is another likely candidate for a soft image.

Fortunately, most image-editing applications have a function that enables you to bring a soft image into sharper focus. The box on the right shows how you can sharpen an image using Elements' *Unsharp Mask;* other applications have similar features. Creating an "unsharp mask" is the process of hiding, or masking, the parts of the image that are unsharp.

Red-Eye
Most cameras have a red-eye option. This involves two flashes: the first makes the subject's pupils contract; the second is the actual exposure. Alternatively, most image-editing applications have options for removing red-eye, and Photoshop Elements' approach, shown on page 37, is typical.

SHARPENING USING *UNSHARP MASK*

▶ Select *Unsharp Mask* from the *Filters* menu. Drag the *Amount* slider up to 400% and the other two sliders to the left. Gradually drag the *Radius* slider to the right until the sharpening effect is visible. Then fine-tune the effect using the *Threshold* slider. Reduce the *Amount* percentage if the result is too extreme.

The before-and-after effect.

▶ Ensure that the image and the thumbnail in the *Unsharp Mask* dialog box are both set to 100% before sharpening, and click the Preview on and off to see the effect on the original image. Sharpening affects the entire image, so use it with care.

FIXING RED-EYE

▲ This shot was taken without red-eye having first been selected from the camera menu. But it can still be fixed even after the photo has been taken.

The *Recipe* palette has a *Remove red eye* option that partly automates the process. The first step is to zoom in to the eye area.

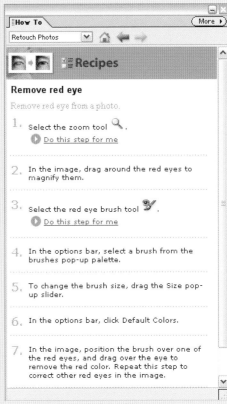

Recipes

Remove red eye
Remove red eye from a photo.

1. Select the zoom tool 🔍.
   ▶ Do this step for me

2. In the image, drag around the red eyes to magnify them.

3. Select the red eye brush tool ✍.
   ▶ Do this step for me

4. In the options bar, select a brush from the brushes pop-up palette.

5. To change the brush size, drag the Size pop-up slider.

6. In the options bar, click Default Colors.

7. In the image, position the brush over one of the red eyes, and drag over the eye to remove the red color. Repeat this step to correct other red eyes in the image.

◀ ▲ Next, select the *Red Eye Brush* tool from the *Tools* palette. Change the brush size so that it is just a little larger than the red-eye area. Select a round brush from the *Default Brushes*. Click the *Default Colors* button, but leave the other options unchanged.

◀ With the *Red Eye Brush,* click on the offending areas until they have been removed. If the brush is too big or you stray beyond the red eyes, you will notice that these areas turn gray, since the *Red Eye* tool takes away color, or "desaturates," anything that it comes into contact with.

Layers

Normal   Opacity: 100%

Lock:

More ▶

✓ Close Palette to Palette Well

Help Contents

Help

using layers

Layers are an essential part of any image-editing program. They enable you to place images on top of one another while also controlling how transparent the layers are. For example, layers enable you to place a photograph on top of a background image and then a border on top of that.

CREATING AND USING LAYERS

1 When you open a new document, you'll notice that there are no layers, just a *Background* layer that cannot be moved from the bottom of the stacking order when layers are added.

2 To create a new layer, click on the *Create a new layer* icon at the bottom of the *Layers* palette (in the circle).

3 Alternatively, select the *Background* or any existing layer and then paste in an image. A new layer will be created automatically.

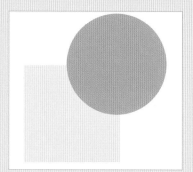

4 On a new layer, draw a square using the *Rectangular Marquee* tool and fill it with yellow using the *Paint Bucket* tool.

5 Use the *Elliptical Marquee* to make a blue circle on another new layer. In the *Layers* palette you'll see the square on *Layer 1* and the circle on *Layer 2*.

6 To turn a layer off (make it invisible), click on the eye icon in the left-hand column and it will disappear from your screen.

7 The selection of an image on one layer can be used to alter the image on a different layer.

8 Using the *Magic Wand* tool, click on the blue circle to select it. Turn off *Layer 2* and select *Layer 1*.

9 Hit the Delete (backspace) key, and a circular portion of the yellow square is removed.

10 A layer is made semitransparent by altering the *Opacity* slider. The effect applies to all layers beneath it.

11 The layer *Blending Mode* is *Normal* by default. Other options alter the way layers interact with each other.

12 A text layer behaves like other layers, but the image thumbnail is replaced with a "T" icon.

13 Clicking the *Link* icon links other layers to the one selected, enabling all to be moved together.

14 The *More* button reveals other options. *Simplify* is used to change a text layer into a graphic. It will no longer be editable, but additional effects can be applied to it.

15 *Merge Visible* will condense all visible layers into one new layer that assumes the identity of the topmost layer. Ensure that the background is not visible when you do this.

getting perfect prints

Printers, like scanners, are supplied with their own software, each featuring preferences that enable you to select print size and shape, resolution, and paper type. To obtain the best-quality printing, it is necessary to understand at least some of the models.

Each time you print from an application, you are able to select options such as paper size and quality. You can also change the default settings so that the options selected always appear as your first choice. In Windows XP, these options can be found in the *Printer Properties*. For Mac OS X, the printing options have to be set for each application individually.

To get the best quality from an inkjet printer, it is essential to select from the *Media* menu the paper type that matches the paper in your printer. The *Quality* settings usually control the resolution, typically ranging from 360 to 1,440 dpi. There is little point in using the *Draft Quality* setting (360 dpi) on expensive photo-quality glossy paper. Conversely, do not try to print *Best Quality* on inexpensive photocopy paper.

Most printer manufacturers sell their own range of papers. They are often more expensive than generic ranges of paper, but the print quality is guaranteed. Compatible ink cartridges rather than branded ones are also available. Although the quality is often very good, some features may be missing. Don't be surprised if, for example, the ink-usage indicator disappears when a less-expensive (non-branded) cartridge is used.

A typical Mac OS X Print dialog. The main options are found in the Print Settings drop-down menu.

A typical Windows XP Printer Properties dialog box. The only tab that needs configuring is Printing Preferences, where you can change the print quality and paper quality and size. Most other options will have been configured during the printer installation and will not need to be changed.

image editing and printing

MATCHING PRINTER AND PAPER

The *Printing Preferences* have to be reset each time a
different paper size or print quality is required. Here, a
4 x 6-in. (10 x 15-cm) perforated photo paper has been
selected (instead of the default letter, 8.5 x 11-in. [A4] size).

▲ Put the new paper into the printer paper tray and adjust the
guides to fit. Select *4 x 6-in. Perforated* from the *Paper Options*
drop-down menu. Check that *Orientation* is correct—either
Portrait or *Landscape*.

▲ Select *Glossy Photo Paper* from the *Paper Options* drop-down
menu and select *Best Photo* from *Quality Type*.

APPLICATION-SPECIFIC PRINT OPTIONS

In addition to the options provided by the printer's software,
some applications provide other features to make printing easier.

▲ *Print Preview* in Photoshop Elements displays the image to be
printed. It has a *Scale to fit Media* option that reduces the image
to fit the paper size.

▲ Paper size and orientation can be changed using the
Page Setup button. If you want to access the full range
of printer settings, hit the *Printer* button.

printing at the right resolution

Modern desktop printers offer fantastic quality, yet people are often disappointed with the results. The maxim "You get out only what you put in" certainly applies to printing. Assuming that your printer preferences are correctly set up to match the paper quality that you are using (see pages 40–41), the problem is likely to be with the image you are printing. One of the most common problems originates with your camera settings. To get as many photos on a disk as possible, your digital camera may be configured with the lowest-quality settings selected. This means that image resolution will be low, and because the files are highly compressed, this means file sizes are smaller, so less valuable memory is used up.

Unless you are using a professional camera, your photos will be saved in .JPG (JPEG) format (see page 15). When a JPEG image is compressed, some of the image content is lost. This is sometimes referred to as a "lossy" process. There are some lossless formats, like TIFF, but these allow for only a modest amount of compression. You may not realize that you are using a substandard image, as it may look all right on screen. If you are unsure, zoom the image to 100% in Elements or any other imaging application. If you see obvious pixelation—that is, blockiness or jaggedy edges rather then smooth tones—you may have a problem.

The problem is compounded when a poor-quality image is rescaled. Ideally, no photographic image should ever be enlarged because this almost always results in a drop in quality. However, a good-quality uncompressed image can usually stand some degree of enlargement. Up to 25% is reasonable for output on a desktop printer. The higher the resolution of the printer, the more obvious the deficiencies will be in the original picture.

If you are uncertain about your camera's quality setup, open a new letter, 8.5 x 11-in. (A4), document in Elements with the resolution set to 200 ppi (good quality) and paste in an image from your camera. If it fills the entire area or beyond, you are probably all right; if the image is much smaller, you should try changing your camera settings.

Most of the projects in this book have been set up with a resolution of 200 ppi. Many experts will tell you this should be 300 ppi, which is fine for professionals using images with high-end commercial printing systems—300 ppi files are much larger, take up more disk space, and may slow an older computer down, but for desktop printing, 200 ppi should suffice.

getting technical

Building blocks

The problems discussed on this page occur because all digital images are made from tiny square blocks called pixels. In this detail, there are about 4,900 pixels (70 across x 70 down). Each one has recorded a fragment of color information. It is easy to see how an image can become pixelated when enlarged. Add to this the problems arising from compression. What JPEG does is to look at the image and decide that a particular group of pixels are so close in color that no one will notice if they all become the same color. Use the lowest resolution setting on your camera only if you can be sure your images will only be viewed on-screen; otherwise use fine or medium settings.

PIXELS PER INCH AND QUALITY SETTINGS

300PPI/10.9 MB

200PPI/4.85 MB

100PPI/1.21 MB

▲ The three images, right, demonstrate how print resolution, image size, and file size are connected. Running top to bottom, we see how a 300 ppi (pixels per inch) image, then a 200 ppi image, and finally a 100 ppi image appear when printed at exactly the same size. As the higher-resolution image (300 ppi, top) has more pixels to every inch, it actually occupies a smaller area but is of better image quality as more pixels are used.

MAXIMUM   MEDIUM   LOW

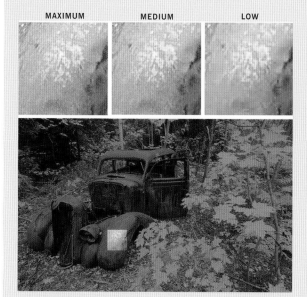

▲ The three enlarged details from the car's fender have been saved in JPEG format at maximum, medium, and low quality. The degradation of image quality is quite small for medium quality but very marked at low quality.

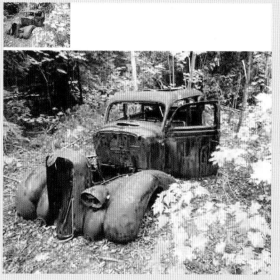

▲ This JPEG image saved at low quality looks all right when small, but when enlarged about five times, it looks very poor. This is the trade-off for a small file size.

ImageStation.

Get yours here.

CART HELP SIGN IN SO

SEARCH

Albums

Picture Gifts   Photo Books   Photo Book - Laminated Portrait

Sony Store

New Album. Print a Photo Book   Already working on a project?
Laminated Portrait

home printing vs. print shop

Anyone using this book to create projects is likely to have a desktop color printer that prints high-quality images at a reasonable price. So why even consider using a professional printing service? Well, you may want a poster-size print for a celebration or some personalized coffee mugs to be used as gifts. Maybe you want the images laminated or professionally mounted, so why not let the supplier print them out as well? The Special Print Projects section (*pages 92–107*) looks at these options in greater detail.

know your equipment

PAPER TYPES

In addition to branded printer manufacture papers, there is a wide variety of generic and specialty papers available. To give an idea of the range and variety, we have listed a selection below. Always check with your supplier to ensure that the paper is compatible with your particular printer—not just the make, but the model, too.

- audiocassette J-card inserts
- backlit film for inkjet printers
- banner paper for inkjet printers
- bookmarks brochure paper
- tri-folds card stock
- bumper stickers & stickers
- business cards
- canvas paper for inkjet printers
- CD stomper labels
- decal paper
- embossing card stock for inkjet printers
- fuzzy paper velour for inkjet printers
- glow-in-the-dark inkjet paper
- greeting card envelopes
- greeting cards
- index cards
- iron-on transfers for fabrics and T-shirts

- jigsaw puzzles for inkjet printers
- key rings
- address labels & shipping labels for inkjet printers
- circular labels for inkjet printers
- VHS face and spine labels for inkjet printers
- magnetic sheets for inkjet printers
- matte inkjet paper coated on one or both sides
- metallic inkjet paper
- overhead transparency film
- painter's canvas
- pearl essence art paper
- photo-quality, water-resistant, inkjet photo paper & card stock
- photo-quality, inkjet paper
- glossy photo quality

- photo base, high gloss inkjet paper
- photo quality, premium grade, inkjet paper glossy
- photo-quality, professional grade, high-gloss, water resistant, inkjet photo paper
- place cards for inkjet printers
- postcards for inkjet printers
- return address labels
- shrink art for color inkjet printers
- T-shirt transfers–Kodak inkjet photo transfers
- table talkers
- table tent card stock tattoos
- vellum envelopes vellum paper
- window decals

The two areas in which your desktop printer may be deficient is print size and paper weight (thickness). The standard paper size for most printers, whether inkjet or laser, is letter, 8.5 x 11 in. (A4), but many models will also print tabloid, 17 x 11-in. (A3), format. Some have a roll-feed attachment that enables banner printing. In part, the paper's weight problem relates to the fact that most desktop printers are compact, and a stiff sheet of card is not supple enough to bend its way round the rollers.

Many established names offer online printing services, and most offer online sharing (*see page 122*). You can upload your images via the Internet, display them on free Web pages, and use those same images to print from—the supplier will mail them to your home. The downside is that these services supply straightforward prints much as old-fashioned film-processing services do instead of the sort of projects included in this book.

Some supermarkets and malls offer printing and even scanning facilities. Some will even burn a CD of your scans for you. This is an option if you don't own a scanner. You will be limited to scanning two-dimensional images, unlike the buttons project on page 49.

Despite these developments, it is likely that most of your printing will be done at home. As well as stand-alone printers, multifunction devices are now very popular. These combine scanner, printer, copier, and sometimes fax and e-mail as well for little more than the cost of a mid-range printer.

MSN PHOTOS

▲ Microsoft has a well-established online printing service. It can be used in combination with MSN Groups that enable online sharing of photos.

Once you have joined or started your own group (online community) and uploaded your photos, you can have them printed and mailed to you at any time.

KODAK PRINT SERVICE

▲ Kodak has similar services: one for Windows XP users, called Ofoto, and one for Mac OS X users, accessed from iPhoto.

IMAGESTATION

▲ Sony's ImageStation has gone one better. As well as providing a service comparable to MSN and Kodak's,

ImageStation also offers a service to create a bound book with your photos printed inside.

print projects

The projects in this chapter can be created using almost any digital-imaging applications. We chose to use Adobe Photoshop Elements, which we have illustrated in the how-to instructions. Follow the step-by-step directions, and you will be surprised how easy it is to achieve professional-looking results. Most of these projects have been designed to be printed on letter, 8.5 x 11-in. (A4) paper, the paper size your printer is most likely to use, but one or two projects have been set up to be printed on tabloid, 11 x 17-in. (A3) paper. For these, we recommend you go to your nearest print shop with the file on a disk and ask for a tabloid, 11 x 17-in. (A3) print. You'll be pleased with how great your work can look at twice its normal size.

IN THIS CHAPTER . . .

borders and backgrounds

There are many ways to add borders and backgrounds to your projects. One of them is to use traditional craft methods. Alternatively, borders can be scanned in as complete images and combined with your photos in an application such as Photoshop Elements.

Here we're going to show you how to create an attractive border or background by using small, individual objects such as buttons, postage stamps, or pressed flowers (*see pages 49–51*). These items can be scanned in and combined with your photos using the computer to create an attractive image. You also have the option of creating borders and frames using Photoshop Elements. You can use the program's presets to fill an area with a pattern or texture, or you can use the *Clone Stamp* tool (*see page 50*) to create a less-regular effect.

If you plan to frame the completed project, it is sensible to buy or make the frame first so you know what size to make the border, background, and photo. In that way, all the components will fit together neatly. Let's start by scanning some buttons.

know your equipment

SCANNER SETTINGS

Each scanner uses slightly different software, so the interface of your scanner may not look the same as the one shown opposite. Don't be alarmed; the majority of settings can be left as default. Resolution is the crucial setting. For most tasks, 150 dpi is sufficient. If you are scanning a small item, a higher resolution may be required, so the image can retain a good level of detail if increased in size later (*see pages 22–23*).

SCANNING REAL BUTTONS

1 Before you arrange the buttons on the scanner glass, ensure they are arranged to fit your finished piece. Here we are using measurements of 8.5 x 11 in. (21.5 x 28 cm), which leaves a small margin at the bottom. (Scanners are designed to accept both a U.S. letter-size document as well as European A4, which is slightly deeper but narrower.) Do not close the scanner lid. Instead, place a sheet of white paper over the top; otherwise the background will be black. Scan using default settings, but set the dpi to 150 and select color. Save the scanned image and open it in Elements.

2 Although placing white paper over the buttons stops the background from going black, it does not produce a clean white background. To achieve this, duplicate the layer by dragging it onto the *Create New Layer* icon at the bottom of the menu.

3 From the *Enhance* menu, select *Adjust Color>Replace Color*. Select the *Eyedropper* tool and sample the off-white color at the center of the image. Set *Fuzziness* to 59 and *Lightness* to +75. This lightens the image, especially the background.

4 The buttons on the layer we have just created are a bit too light, so reduce *Opacity* to 50% and change the *Layer Blending* mode to *Hard Light*. This lets some of the original layer show through and puts the richness of color back into the buttons.

5 The final border image is now ready to receive a photo.

SCANNING A SMALL FLOWER

① Choose a flower to scan. We've used a small pink flower and scanned it at 400 dpi so that the image can be increased in size without losing detail. This time, do not cover it with white paper, as the black background can be used to help "cut out" the flower. Once scanned, open the image in Elements. Select the *Magic Wand* tool from *Tools* and click the black area. A selection will appear around the edge of the flower (dotted line). Adjust *Tolerance* in *Options* until the selection fits tightly.

② Invert the selection so it selects the flower rather than the background. Then select *Copy* from the *Edit* menu. Open a new document (here we've chosen letter, 8.5 x 11-in. (A4) again) and paste the flower into it.

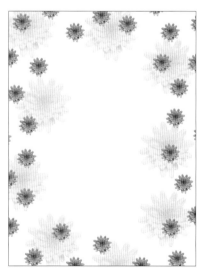

③ Drag the flower image to the top left of the page and reduce the size a little (if you wish) by clicking on one of the bounding box corners and dragging it toward the center. From the *Tools* menu, select the *Clone Stamp* tool. From the *Options* menu, select a *Hard Round* brush and adjust the size so that it is a little bigger than the flower.

④ Place the cursor (which will now be the size of the brush that you specified) over the flower. With the *Alt* key pressed, click once. This loads the cursor with the cloned image. Move to an area where you want to place another flower and click again. This copies the cloned image in that place. Repeat this until you have covered the area that you require.

⑤ Create a new layer and paste in the flower image again, but this time make it larger and reduce the layer *Opacity* to 28%. Repeat the process of Clone Stamping, but don't forget to enlarge the brush size.

ADDING PATTERNS

Elements lets you fill areas with patterns. There are many presets, but creating a custom pattern is easy. We've used a motif scanned from a Christmas card. Open a new 1.7 x 1.7-in. (4.3 x 4.3 cm) document with a transparent background. This way the pattern will repeat five times and fill the width of the page—5 x 1.7 in. = 8.5 in. (5 x 4.3 cm = 21.5 cm). Paste two copies of the image —one top-left, the other bottom-right, to give a wallpaper effect when the pattern is applied.

From the *Edit* menu, select *Define Pattern* and give it a name when prompted. This pattern is now stored for you to use in future projects. Once that's done, open a new page (letter, 8.5 x 11 in. (A4) again) and create a new layer. Select the *Paint Bucket* tool from the *Tools* menu, and select *Pattern* from the *Options* bar. The new pattern will appear at the bottom of the drop-down menu. Next, use the *Paint Bucket* tool to fill the newly created layer with your pattern.

Add a new layer below the pattern layer. Using the *Paint Bucket* tool, fill it with a color of your choice. Reset the *Fill* options on the *Options* bar to *Foreground,* or the area will fill with the pattern again.

To convert the overall background to a border, simply add a new layer above the others. Using the *Rectangular Marquee* tool from the *Tools* menu, define an area and then fill it with white.

In order to give the border some depth, go to the *Bevels* menu in the *Layer Styles* palette, then select *Simple Sharp Pillow Emboss.*

greeting card

This project was inspired by a snapshot of the photographer's daughter after a sleepover with friends. The addition of her favorite teddy bear required an extra photo, which was shot (without flash) on a summer afternoon. The text adds to the charm of the shot, since it appears to be spoken by the bear rather than the child.

When making a greeting card, you will have to work back from the envelope size you plan to use. For this project, we have chosen a U.S. A2-size envelope—4⅜ x 5¾ in. (11 x 14.5 cm). The greeting card is a standard inkjet card size of 8 x 5 in. (20 x 13 cm), folding once to become 4 x 5 in. (10 x 13 cm). The ideal size to fit the envelope is a fraction larger, at 8½ x 5½ in. (21.5 x 14 cm), folding once to become 4¼ x 5½ in. (10.75 x 14 cm). However, this is not an inkjet card size. You can, of course, print on a larger size card and trim it down afterward if you wish. When matching standard printer paper sizes to an envelope, try cutting a piece of folded scrap paper to the paper size before starting the project to check whether it will fit the envelope comfortably.

The outside of the card will be printed with the front image on the right-hand side so that it is in the correct position when folded; the same applies to the message on the reverse side. Unless your printer has a duplex printing facility (enabling it to print on both sides of the paper at once), you will have to print the two faces of the card separately. When printing the reverse side, take care to insert the card into the printer with the correct orientation. The card's thickness is defined by weight. A typical weight of card will be 50 lb/185 gsm. Not all cards and papers are suitable for double-sided printing, so check this with your supplier before you start.

The finished thank you card ready to send out to friends and their bears.

TEDDY BEAR GREETING CARD

In this example, we'll be showing you how to combine two photos together to make a greeting card, and how to add your own text—and text effects—to the card.

① The shot of the teddy bear was taken against a plain background so the image could be easily cut out. From the *Tools* menu, pick the *Magnetic Lasso* tool and trace around the bear. Use the *Edge Contrast* setting in the *Options Bar* to better control the selection. The lower the contrast between the object and the background, the lower this setting should be.

② Once you've completed the selection, choose the *Feather* option from the *Select* menu and set the *Feather Radius* to about 3 pixels. This will create a softer edge when the image is cut out. Setting this can be a case of trial and error. As a rule, the higher the image resolution, the greater the radius will have to be to obtain the same effect.

③ From the *Select* menu, choose *Inverse* and then use *Edit>Cut* to remove the background, leaving only the bear. The image is now ready to be added to the card.

④ Since the photo is smaller than the size of our greeting card, create a new 8 x 5-in. (20 x 13-cm) document for your card with a resolution between 150 and 300 ppi (pixels per inch). Create a new layer (Layer 1) and use the *Fill* tool to fill it with black. Then change the layer *Opacity* to about 65%. continued ▶▶

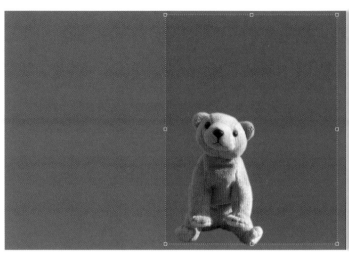

⑤ Create another new layer (Layer 2). Using the *Rectangular Marquee* tool, define an area on the right half of the page that leaves about a quarter-inch margin around what will be the front face of the card. Fill this area with black again, and this time change the *Opacity* to 25%.

⑥ Return to the bear document. Choose *All* from the *Select* menu and then *Copy* from the *Edit* menu. Next, return again to the card document and paste the bear image above the other layers.

⑦ Open the image of the child. Using the *Rectangular Marquee* tool from the *Tools* menu, select the area of the image that you wish to use and then select *Copy* from the *Edit* menu. Return again to the card document and paste the image immediately below the layer containing the bear.

⑧ Select the layer created in step 4 (Layer 1), and create a new adjustment layer by clicking the icon at the base of the *Layers* palette. Then select *Hue/Saturation*. Check the *Colorize* button and adjust the three sliders (*Hue*, *Saturation*, and *Brightness*) to create your desired color. The adjustment layer enables you to experiment with colors without affecting the original image. Select the layer created in step 5 (Layer 2) and change the *Layer Blending Mode* to *Overlay*. This lets more of the orange come through.

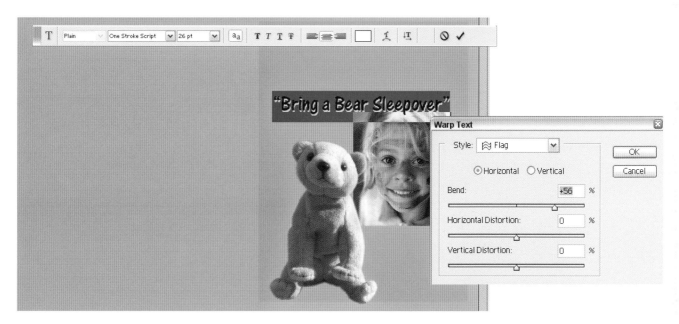

Now you can add the "Bring a Bear Sleepover" text. Select the *Horizontal Type* tool from the *Tools* palette and then create a new layer, and type in the text. The font will depend on those available on your computer. Select *Create Warped Text* from the *Options* bar and choose the *Flag* style. Create the remaining paragraphs of text in the same way, but on two additional layers and without warping the text.

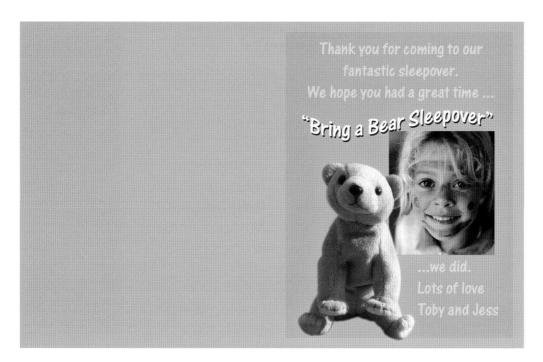

The finished card front will have to be folded when printed. If you lightly score the inside with a craft knife, this will help you achieve a clean, unbuckled fold. If you want to print a message on the reverse, set up another identically sized document, create the graphics, then print on the reverse side.

birthday invitation

This project shows how easy it is to create a special effect like combining a child's head with an animal's body for an innovative birthday invitation.

Provided that both the child's and the animal's faces have been photographed from the same angle (preferably front-on, as here), Photoshop Elements will make light work of this task.

The technique is to use Elements' feathered selection (*see step 3 and tip box on page 57*). This enables you to create a seamless blend between the two photos. If you intend to use 6 x 4-in. (15 x 10-cm) perforated cards on which to print the invitations, remember to position all the visual elements to allow for the area outside the perforation to be removed (*see step 10*).

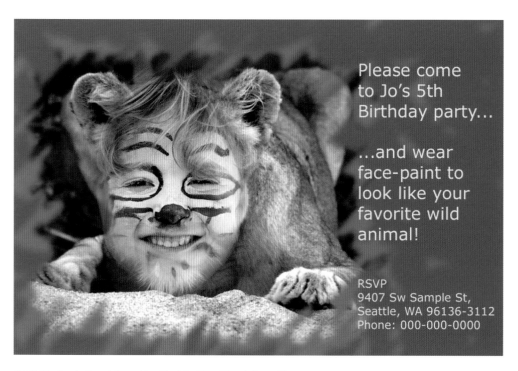

Please come to Jo's 5th Birthday party...

...and wear face-paint to look like your favorite wild animal!

RSVP
9407 Sw Sample St,
Seattle, WA 96136-3112
Phone: 000-000-0000

The finished project was trimmed to a 6 x 4-in. (15 x 10-cm) shape. Since this card will be mailed, it is sensible to give it waterproof protection using a spray available from your paper suppliers (be sure to follow instructions closely). The addressee details can be written on the reverse.

COMBINING THE IMAGES

Select *New* from the *File* menu. Create a new 7 x 4.5-in. (18 x 11.5-cm) document with a resolution of 200 ppi.

Paste the wild animal and the child's face photos into the new document. Use the corner handles to reduce each image to a convenient size.

If the angles of the two faces don't match, as here, use the corner handles to rotate the child's face to match the lion. Make sure that the layer with the child's face is selected in the *Layers* palette.

→ tip

Feathering a selection ensures that any selection made doesn't have a hard edge to it. This helps when you are combining images, since it helps to blend one image into another. The higher the radius of the feathering, the "softer" the edge becomes.

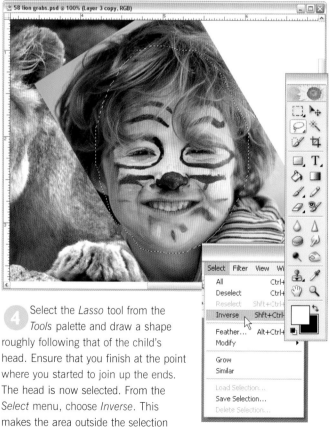

Select the *Lasso* tool from the *Tools* palette and draw a shape roughly following that of the child's head. Ensure that you finish at the point where you started to join up the ends. The head is now selected. From the *Select* menu, choose *Inverse*. This makes the area outside the selection active rather than the head.

continued ▶▶

COMBINING THE IMAGES – CONTINUED

5 From the *Select* menu, choose *Feather* and set the *Feather Radius* to 30 pixels. Now hit the keyboard Delete key or use *Clear* from the *Edit* menu. The background has been removed from the child's face. It may be necessary to use Delete or *Clear* a second time to fully remove the background.

6 Using *Feather* in the previous step means that there is a soft, semitransparent "feather" around the shape rather than a hard edge. This lets part of the image below show through. Now drag the child's face over the lion's face. Adjust the size and position using the corner handles.

ADDING A JUNGLE FRAME

7 Select the *Brush* tool from the *Tools* palette. Then select *Calligraphic Brushes* from the *Options* bar and choose 77 pixels as the size. Select the *Foreground Color* from the *Tools* palette and make this green. Roughly draw in the jungle background on a new layer above the others.

8 From the *Filters* drop-down menu, select *Blur>Gaussian Blur* and adjust the *Radius* to about 7 pixels. The effect we are trying to simulate is looking through jungle leaves. Blurring helps to achieve this.

58 **print projects**

9 On a new layer above the others, repeat the drawing and blurring described in steps 7 and 8. This time, however, make the *Foreground Color* a little darker and don't fill in so much of the area.

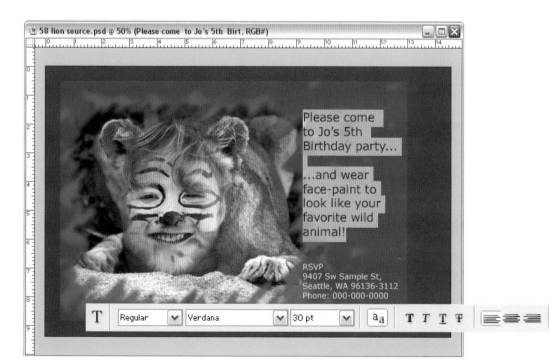

10 On a new layer above the others, select the *Horizontal Type* tool from the *Tools* palette and type in the message. We used Verdana at a point size of 30 in a pale yellow color, which was sampled from the child's face using the *Eyedropper* tool. We reduced the font size to 20 point for the address details. If you are printing on 6 x 4-in. (10 x 15-cm) perforated cards, keep the text within the area indicated by the darker border.

place cards

Creating place cards is a quick and easy project. All you need are some photographs of the friends you've invited to your dinner party and you're all set.

Cropping tightly into the face is more fun and dynamic than using a standard full portrait. If you want to be really radical, you could crop in farther to a facial detail like the eye or mouth so the individual's identity is further disguised. Assembling all the photos as individual layers in one Elements document makes it easier to rescale and position them consistently. As most inkjet printers do not print to the edge of the paper, we have chosen to use a perforated 6 x 4-in. (15 x 10-cm) photo paper. This is slightly oversize so that when the perforated waste is torn off, the print will be exactly 6 x 4-in. (15 x 10-cm). If you prefer, use a larger size paper without perforations and then trim back to the required size.

As a finishing touch, you could round off the corners with a craft knife. Finally, place the cards in position on the table. All you have to do now is prepare the meal!

PREPARING THE IMAGES

Using Elements' *File Browser*, select the photos that you intend to use for the project. Drag them onto the main window, and they will open automatically.

Select *New* from the *File* menu and create a new document 7 x 4.5-in, with a resolution of 200 ppi.

Using the *Move* tool, click on one of the photos and drag it onto the empty document that you have just created. This copies the image as a new layer. As the new document is smaller than the original and is also a landscape format, the image is cropped—just what was intended.

continued ▶▶

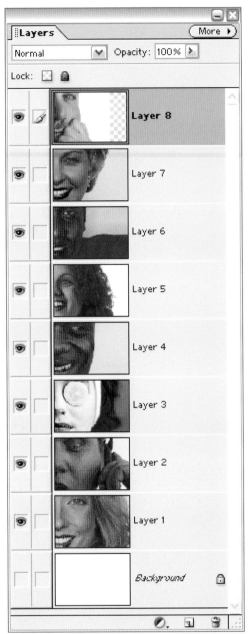

4 Drag the second image into the new document. Because the face is bigger, it needs to be reduced so that it is about the same size as the first one. If you zoom out to 25%, the full extent of the original image will be visible. From the *Image* menu, select *Transform Image>Free Transform* and rescale using the corner handles. As you resize, hold the *Shift* key down to constrain the image to its original proportions.

Some images will need to be rotated to ensure the eyes are horizontal. Use *Free Transform* again. This time, positioning the cursor just outside the corner changes it to a *Rotate* icon. Use this to align the eyes. If necessary, the entire image can be moved by dragging from the center point.

5 When all eight images are positioned, the *Layers* palette will look like this. Turn off the *Background* using the *Eye* icon. This will show you if any of the images on the other layers aren't big enough to cover the image area—as shown in *Layer 8* above.

6 Layer 8 needs some background added. Use the *Eyedropper* tool to sample the white background. This will now become the active *Foreground color*. Use a conveniently sized brush to paint over the area.

→tip

Using templates

An alternative method of printing place cards from Elements is to use a blank MS Word document pre-formatted to enable two 6 x 4-in. (15 x 10-cm) cards to be printed on a single letter-size card. You can download these templates from companies like Avery (http://www.avery.com). Print on a perforated card supplied by the same manufacturer to ensure an exact fit.

7 Printing on perforated 6 x 4-in. (15 x 10-cm) photo paper means 0.25 in. (0.5 cm) of the image will be trimmed off top and bottom and 0.5 in (1 cm). off either end. To account for this, each face will have to be moved a similar distance to the right so that it is trimmed between the eyes. Turn on the required layer before printing, and remember to turn the others off.

vacation album

For this project, you will need to download one of the master file templates, Vacation Album Special.psd or Vacation Album Plain.psd from our web-linked website (full address to the right).

These vacation album templates can be downloaded from the web-linked site www.prdpus.web-linked.com as letter, 8.5 x 11-in. (A4), documents. You will be able to add your own photographs, then type in a new title and captions. If you decide to use the "Plain" version (*see page 67*), you will be able to add your own colors and effects. To give your project a more professional look, create a title that connects to your main photo.

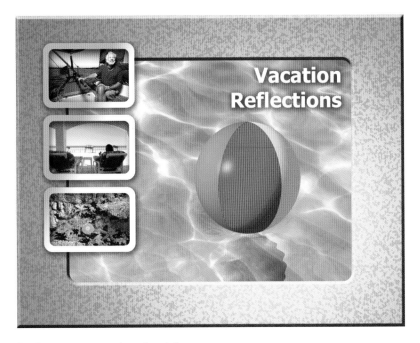

Creating your own personal vacation photo album enables you to add text directly onto the printed pages, giving you the opportunity to add details and captions at will.

→ tip

printing layers

As you create more pages and thus more layers, it is preferable to print each page when you finish it. You can then turn off the unwanted images and add those intended for the next page. Of course, any layer can be turned on subsequently if you want to reprint it. If you find it tiresome working with many layers, use the *Save As* command to create a carbon copy of the document and work on that as well. Always remember to use *Save* before *Save As,* or only the new document will reflect the changes made since you last saved it.

USING THE TEMPLATE

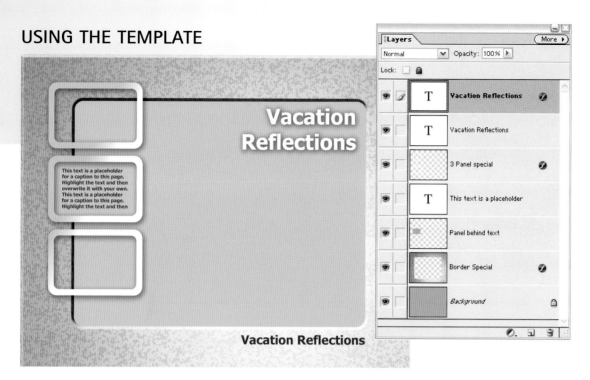

If using the Vacation Album Special.psd document, the screen shot will show one large panel and three smaller ones. Two layers, *Panel behind text* and *This text is a placeholder,* are currently visible. These can be turned on or off, depending on whether you want to add text or another image.

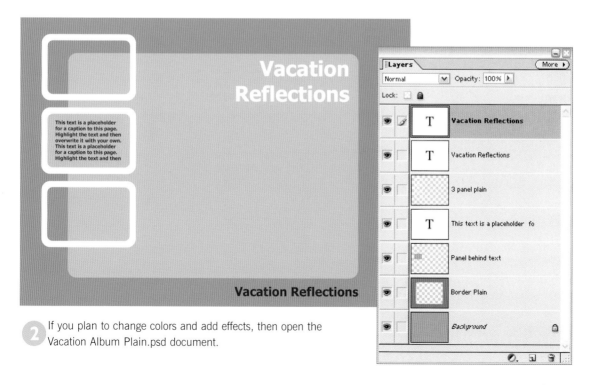

If you plan to change colors and add effects, then open the Vacation Album Plain.psd document.

continued ▶▶

End of another glorious day

3 Open and copy the photo you want to use as your main image. Open Vacation Album Special.psd and turn off the *Panel behind text* and *This text is a placeholder* layers. Create a new layer and drag it below the *Border* layer and paste your image. Use the *Transform* handles to resize and position it. Create another new layer and drag it below the *3 Panel* layer. As you did before, copy, paste, resize, and position three smaller photos within the three frames. This completes page one.

4 Page two shows the *Panel behind text* and *This text is a placeholder* layers turned on. Add your own text here. New photos have been added so that they appear behind the two remaining panels. A new main image has been added below the *Border* layer. The main title layer has been turned off and the smaller one (bottom right) turned on.

Land Ahoy!

Food for the stomach and for the soul

5 Page three follows the process described in step 4, but this time the two smaller panels have been left blank. With a rigid design like this, a few pages that are different will make the project more interesting.

6 Page four continues the process of replacing photos and text. Try to give each page a theme. Even if it is somewhat contrived, it will add a professional touch.

ALTERNATIVE TREATMENTS

▲ Here, using Vacation Album Plain.psd, default colors have been retained but the text on *This text is a placeholder* layer has moved to the top panel. The *Panel behind text* layer has been turned off so the corner of the image shows through.

▲ The theme here is obviously relaxation in the sun. Using candid shots gives your project an intimacy usually missing from posed ones. Select a color scheme that reinforces the effect.

TIP

If you would like to customize your album, there are endless possibilities with the Vacation Album Plain.psd. Just let your imagination and creative flair roam free.

▲ This album format can be used for any subject, not only vacations. Here it is used to display a collection of photos of the humble bench. One image has been split between two frames. The text has been changed to white and moved into the main frame. Create the border effect by selecting *Complex>White Grid* from the *Layer Styles* palette.

family portraits

Here we look at two very different ways of displaying your favorite family portraits. The floral frame uses a traditional border but is presented in a modern manner. The chrome frame is uncompromisingly contemporary. It uses a shape reminiscent of a classic-car radiator or perhaps a piece of modern jewelry.

Both these projects make extensive use of Photoshop Elements' *Layer Styles*, a terrific feature that lets you choose from many different formats.

Photoshop Elements has numerous filter and layer effects that, when combined together, provide you with an almost infinite number of styles and treatments.

CREATING A FLORAL FRAME

1 If you're going to scan the border from this book, create a new letter, 8.5 x 11-in. (A4), document in Photoshop Elements. Scan the border and paste it into the new document.

2 Alternatively download the border (floral_frame.psd) from the web-linked website (www.prdpus.web-linked.com) and open it in Elements and turn off *Layer 1*.

3 Open your portrait image and copy it. Go back to the frame, create a new layer and paste your portrait image into it. Drag the new image layer below the frame layer.

4 Use the *Transform* handles to scale the image to fit within the oval. Next, reselect the frame layer and from the *Tools* palette select the *Magic Wand* tool. Click inside the oval to create a selection and then choose *Inverse* from the *Select* drop-down menu.

5 With the selection made in step 4 still active, return to the photo layer and hit the Delete key. This removes the unwanted background. Return to the *Select* drop-down menu and *Deselect* the selection.

6 On a new layer below all the others, use the *Paint Bucket* tool to fill the layer with a background color that harmonizes with the photo. The color will show through, as the frame is transparent.

continued ▶▶

To change the color of the black frame, select the frame layer. From the *Enhance* drop-down menu, select *Adjust Color>Hue/Saturation*. On the resulting dialog box, check *Colorize* and move the sliders to the positions shown here. The frame becomes the color shown in the bottom band of the box; here, it is blue. Adjust the sliders to select alternatives.

ALTERNATIVES

These images show the wide range of one-click effects that can be achieved using *Layer Styles*. Apply them after completing step 7.

Soft Edge

Blue Ghost

Inner Ridge

Wow-Chro...

From the *Layer Styles* palette, select *Image Effects>Sun Faded Photo*. The frame will now have a graduated blue blend.

CREATING A CHROME FRAME

1 Download and open chrome_frame.psd from the web-linked site. Turn off *Layer 1* and turn on the frame layer. Open and copy your portrait image, then return to the frame document and paste your image. Next, follow steps 4 and 5 on page 69.

2 Select the frame layer. From the *Layer Styles* palette, select *Wow Chrome>Beveled Edge*. The default setting applies a thin bevel to the frame.

3 Double-click the small *Layer Styles* icon in the frame layer. This opens a *Style Settings* palette. Drag the *Bevel Size* slider up to 65 to increase the bevel size.

4 Select the Background layer. Using the *Paint Bucket* tool, fill the background with black.

5 To complete the effect, select *Patterns>Diamond Plate* from the *Layer Styles* palette.

family tree

This is another project that uses a simple master file template from the web-linked website (www.prdpus.web-linked.com). It has been created as a letter, 8.5 x 11-in. (A4), document.

The family tree template gives you lots of opportunities to personalize a family history that's right for you. You can type in the correct family-member details, and add pictures of each of them if you'd like. Then you can add your own background photo to create a very professional-looking and personalized family tree. The tree includes spaces for you and your partner, your parents, grandparents, great-grandparents, and three children. If you need to add more family members, simply adjust the *Image Placeholder* and *Link Lines* layers.

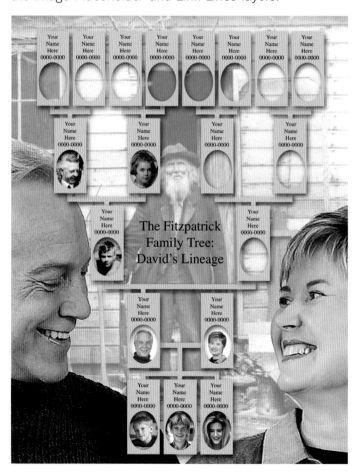

A personalized family tree is great fun to make and will provide you with a unique record of your genealogy that you can share with family and friends.

FAMILY TREE

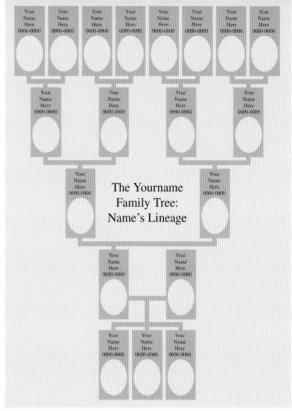

THE MAIN TITLE LAYER ——————

THE 19 TEXT LAYERS, ONE
FOR EACH RELATIVE'S
NAME AND DATES ——————

HUE/SATURATION ADJUSTMENT LAYER
(this applies only to the Image Placeholder) ——

IMAGE PLACEHOLDER LAYER ——————

HUE/SATURATION ADJUSTMENT LAYER
(this applies only to the Link Lines) ——————

LINK LINES LAYER ——————

HUE/SATURATION ADJUSTMENT LAYER
(this applies only to the Background Color) ——————

BACKGROUND COLOR LAYER ——————

BACKGROUND ——————

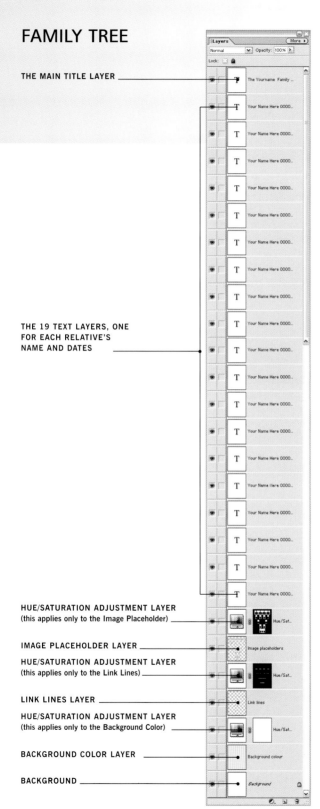

1 Open the Family Tree.psd document. From the *Palette Dock*, drag off the *Layers* palette. This ensures that the *Layers* palette stays open. Expand it to the maximum depth available on your screen. Use the scroll bar to show the layers at the bottom. The master file is ready for you to add your personal details. Clicking the layer thumbnail of any *Hue/Saturation* adjustment layer will open a dialog box that enables you to easily change the color of the layer below it (see *Alternatives box on page 75*).

2 If you wish to repeat the project based on your partner's lineage, use the *Rectangular Marquee* tool to select the link and drag it to the correct position before adding his or her family's details.

continued ▶▶

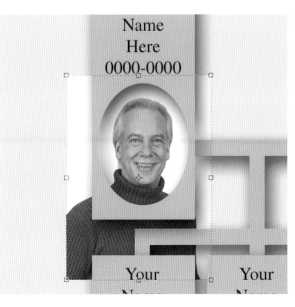

3 With the Image Placeholder layer selected, click on *Drop Shadows>Soft Edge* from the *Layer Styles* palette. Repeat this process for the *Link Lines* layer. Both will now have a shadow behind that "lifts" them from the page.

4 Add a new layer immediately below the *Link Lines* layer and paste in the first photo. Use the *Transform* handles to rescale and reposition it to fit within the frame.

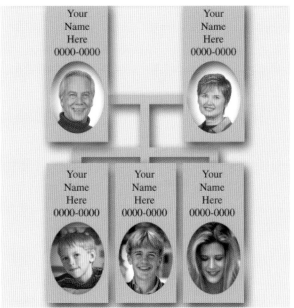

5 To remove the unwanted area of the image, first use the *Rectangular Marquee* tool to define the area. Then choose *Inverse* from the *Select* drop-down menu. Hit the Delete key, and the unwanted area will disappear.

6 Continue adding the remaining photos following the process described above.

FAMILY TREE—CONTINUED

7 When adding previous generations to the project, the images are likely to be black and white. If you wish to add a sepia tone to them, select *Photographic Effects>Sepia Tone* from the *Layer Styles* menu.

8 If you wish to add an overall image to the project, ensure that it is pasted in above the *Background Color* layer. To add color to the image, double-click on the layer thumbnail of the *Hue/Saturation* adjustment layer. You can apply a color (here we have used blue) by using the sliders.

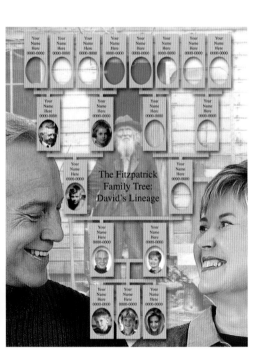

9 You may wish to add an image of yourself and your partner. Paste it into a layer above the layer described above, or this image too will be blue. To enable the image in step 8 to show through, delete the background in the photo of you and your partner *(see pages 31 and 53)*.

ALTERNATIVES

It is very easy to change any of the project colors if you have downloaded the Family Tree.psd document.

Change the color of *Image Placeholder* and *Link Lines* layers by clicking the layer thumbnail of the relevant *Hue/ Saturation* adjustment layer. Here, it has been changed to blue.

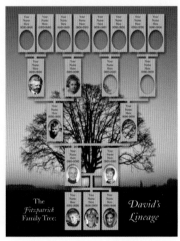

If you prefer to use a darker background image that results in the title being illegible, it could be split into two parts and the color changed to white, as here. If you have access to a wider range of fonts, using an italic one like Caslon creates a professional look.

scrapbook

E.J. is an avid photographer who wants to make the most of images taken over a number of years. Rather than simply grouping images by place or family, E.J. has built a scrapbook based around themes like the one shown here, which features some quirky images of signs.

This scrapbook project was designed to fit on tabloid, 17 x 11-in. (A3) paper, but it can be printed to fit a smaller format if the larger option is not available or if you'd rather not use a print shop. Depending on the binding methods available, the pages can be bound at the left with, for example, a plastic binding strip or staples. Another option is to crease each page 2 inches (5 centimeters) in from the left so that the pages hinge where the blue strip and orange background join.

The next time you go on vacation, think of a theme, such as wildlife, architecture, or neon signs, that you can photograph. These can often make an unusual and unique record of your time away and can add interest to traditional photos of family and friends.

EJ'S DIGITAL PHOTO SCRAPBOOK

Time of the Signs

DIGITAL PHOTO SCRAPBOOK

1 Open a new tabloid, 17 x 11-in. (A3) landscape document in Elements. If your printer is unable to print at this size, select the *Scale to Fit* Media option from the *Print Preview* menu when you want to print the finished project.

2 Assemble the photos that you want to use for the project and paste each of them into the new document. On a new layer below the photos, use the *Rectangular Marquee* tool to create a 2-in. (5-cm)-wide selection on the extreme left and fill with color—we used blue.

3 Use the *Color Picker* to change the foreground color to orange. From the *Tools* palette select the *Pencil* tool, and then in the *Options* bar change the size to 16 pixels. On a new layer hold the Shift key down and draw a horizontal line across the entire width of the document and repeat the process for a vertical line. Use the rulers (*View>Rulers*) to set the lines at 5.5-in. (14-cm) vertical and 9.5-in. (24-cm) horizontal.

4 From the *Layers Styles* palette select *Bevels>Simple Sharp Pillow Emboss*; this gives the lines a 3D effect.

continued ▶▶

5 On a new layer below the border layer, use the *Paint Bucket* tool to fill the layer with the same orange color that you used in step 4.

6 Select *Render/Lens* flare from the *Filter* menu and drag the center cross down to produce a horizontal flare, adjusting the *Brightness* setting to 142. You have now created four equal compartments in which to display your photos.

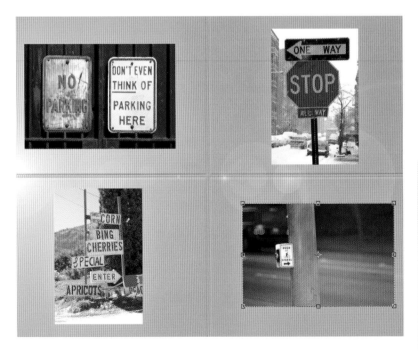

→ tip

Positioning the images

Most printers leave a small margin of white paper around the edge; don't forget to allow for this when positioning the photos. It might be helpful to create a new layer with a 0.25-in. (0.5-cm) margin filled with a contrasting color (for example, red). This layer can be deleted when you have finished positioning the photos.

7 Select and rescale each image to fit comfortably within each compartment. It will look more professional if the image size is consistent.

8 With one of the photos still selected, choose *Drop Shadows/Soft Edge* from the *Layer Styles* menu and repeat this to the other photos.

9 On a new layer (moved to the top) use the *Horizontal Type* tool to type in the title (we used 112 point Garamond Bold), then use the *Transform* handles to rotate the title. Holding down the Shift key will help find the vertical position.

10 Use the *Layers Style* described in step 8 to apply a drop shadow to the title and position it within the blue panel. When you have printed out the first sheet, turn off the four original photo layers and turn on four others. Don't forget to apply the drop shadow to the new ones.

11 For the title page of your scrapbook, select a really strong image and try to match it with a catchy title. A finishing touch is to apply a pattern over the orange background. With the foreground color set to white, from the *Tools* palette choose the *Custom Shape* tool and select *Grass 1* from the *Nature* category. On a new layer, hold down the mouse button and drag the cursor, starting top left to bottom right. From the *Layers* palette select the *More* button and choose *Simplify Layer*, and reduce the *Opacity* to 25%.

photo story

Saving the memories of a family day out is a straightforward task with Elements. This project is enhanced by the addition of the boot-print background and the hand-drawn graphic of the river, both of which are easy to create.

The addition of captions to any photo story helps personalize the result, as we have done here with an example journey along the banks of Cooper's Creek. If you are uneasy about drawing the course of the creek directly in Elements, you could draw it on paper first. Next, scan it and paste it into the Elements document and then, using this as a guide, trace over it on a new layer with the *Brush* tool. This is another tabloid, 17 x 11-in. (A3) project. If your printer is limited to a smaller size, use the *Scale to fit media* option.

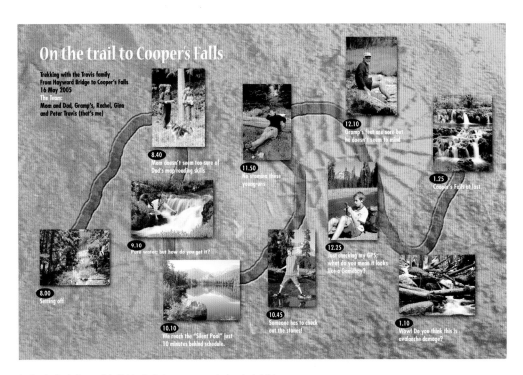

Instead of printing out individual photos as a record of a day's hiking, it's more effective to select the strongest images and place them on one large page with dates, times and, captions that chart the day's events.

COOPER'S CREEK PHOTO STORY

① A boot print in soft sand forms the background to this project. The boot was pressed into a tray of coarse sand. This was photographed without flash, but with an angled lamp providing strong side lighting. The quality of this image is not important, since it will be manipulated in step 3.

② Open a new tabloid, 17 x 11-in. (A3) document in Elements. Paste the boot-print photo into the new document. Using the *Transform* handles, drag it to a convenient size to fill the entire background.

③ Click the *Create new fill or Adjustment Layer* icon at the base of the *Layers* palette. Choose *Hue/Saturation*, then check *Colorize* and drag the sliders to the values shown above. With *Colorize* checked, the image becomes the color shown in the bottom band of the dialog box. In this example, it is a mid-tan color.

④ On a new layer above the previous one, select the *Brush* tool from the *Tools* palette. From the *Options* bar, use a default hard-edged brush, but change the size to about 77 pixels. This will be the thickness of the line. Select a deep blue as the foreground color and draw the river in one fluid movement. If you make a mistake, simply undo and try again.

continued ▶▶

Having assembled the images to be used in this project, paste the first one into position. You will need to reduce the size of each image using the *Transform* handles. Hold the Shift key down while doing so to avoid distorting the image.

Continue pasting and resizing each image until they are all in position.

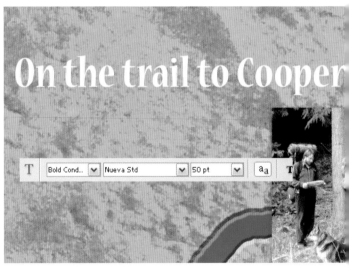

The images that you have pasted in are all on separate layers. Select each layer in turn and, from the *Layer Styles* palette, select *Soft Edge* from the *Drop Shadows* menu.

Create a new layer above the others for the heading text. Use the *Horizontal Type* tool to type in the title. Here, we have used Nueva Bold Condensed at 50 point.

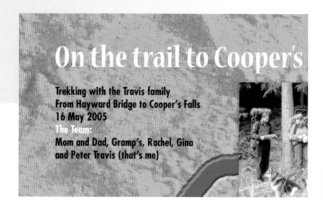

On the trail to Cooper's

**Trekking with the Travis family
From Hayward Bridge to Cooper's Falls
16 May 2005
The Team:
Mom and Dad, Gramp's, Rachel, Gina
and Peter Travis (that's me)**

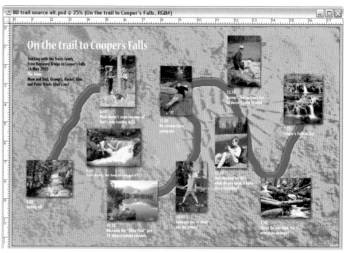

9 Create another new layer above the others. Then use the *Horizontal Type* tool to type in the subhead. Here, we used Futura Bold Condensed at 16 point.

10 On another new layer, add a caption to the first image using the same type style as the previous step. Continue this process until all the captions are complete. As each will be on a new layer, your document will now have a lot of layers. You will have to scroll up and down the *Layers* palette in order to select them.

11 On a new layer below all the caption layers, use the *Elliptical Marquee* tool from the flyout menu on the *Tools* palette and draw an oval. Use the *Paint Bucket* tool to fill it with black. Use the *Magic Wand* to reselect the oval shape and drag it to the next position. Ensure the *Magic Wand* is still selected as you drag the oval. This ensures that the first black oval is not moved as well. Fill the second oval with black, and continue until all are completed.

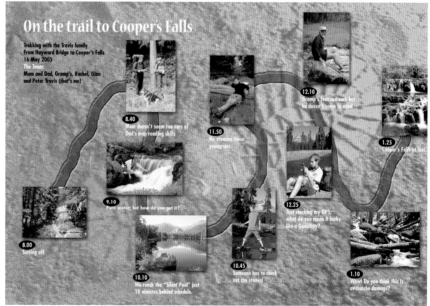

12 As a finishing touch, select the rivers layer and, from the *Layers* palette *Blending Mode* drop-down menu, select *Linear Light* rather than the default *Normal*. This lets some of the background image show through.

calendar

This project was designed as letter, 8.5 x 11-in. (A4) size, but it can be printed to fit a larger tabloid, 11 x 17-in. (A3) format. Before starting, check on the amount of border that your printer leaves; if it is more than a quarter inch, make the frame a little wider than the one inch specified in this project.

The pages for the calendar shown here are assembled in one multilayered Photoshop Elements file. This enables you to easily maintain consistent alignment of text and images. As Elements is an image-editing application, it does not have very sophisticated paragraph text-handling features. To overcome this limitation, the font used for the calendar dates is italic. This makes any slight misalignment of the columns less noticeable than it would be if a regular font were used.

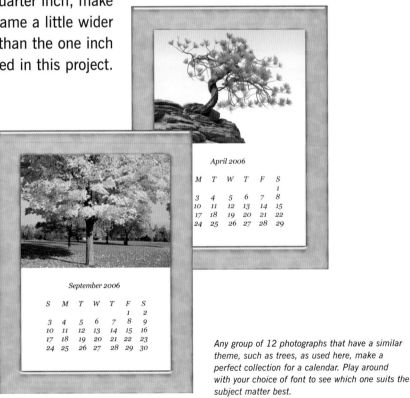

Any group of 12 photographs that have a similar theme, such as trees, as used here, make a perfect collection for a calendar. Play around with your choice of font to see which one suits the subject matter best.

TREES CALENDAR

1. Open a new document in Photoshop Elements using a letter, 8.5 x 11-in. (A4), portrait format.

2. On a new layer using the *Rectangular Marquee* tool, create a selection 1 in. (2.5 cm) in from the edge of the page. Choose *Inverse* from the *Select* menu.

3. Use the *Paint Bucket* tool to fill the selection with black to create a 1-in. (2.5-cm) border around the page.

4. Select *Wow Plastic* from the *Layer Styles* menu. This effect is semi-transparent—a quality that we will use in the next step.

continued ▶▶

5 With the *Brush* tool selected, choose *Falling Ivy Leaves* from the *Options* menu and change the size to 120 pixels.

6 Ensure the foreground color is still set to black, and on a new layer below the frame, use the *Brush* tool to paint in the leaves under the border. It may take a few attempts to get it right. You can add single leaves with one mouse click.

7 Select the border layer, and using the *Magic Wand* tool, make a selection inside the frame. Return to the leaves layer and hit the delete button. This trims away the unwanted leaves.

8 On a new layer (above the frame), paste in the first of the photos to be used to illustrate the months of the year. Repeat the selection process in step 7, but this time choose *Inverse* from the *Select* menu. Hit the Delete button and the excess image will be removed.

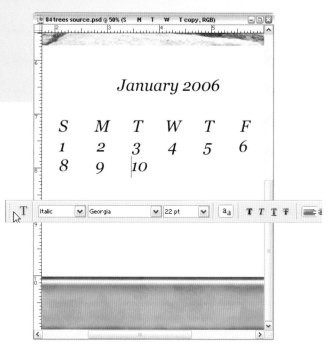

On a new layer select the *Horizontal Type* tool and choose the font Georgia italic at 22 point. Type in the month name. Allow a line space, and then type in the initial letter of each day. As Elements does not have a tab function, use the keyboard space bar to achieve the desired position of each letter. Continue typing in the dates using the same method of alignment.

→ **tip**

Cover page

A cover page is a nice way to finish off the project, especially if it is to be a gift. Since it won't be displayed for long, if at all, a simple typographical page can be used. Here the title is the same as the font used for the dates, but at 88 point. The *Eyedropper* tool has been used to sample a pale brown from the frame.

Adjust the position of the date text so that it sits comfortably beneath the photo and then repeat the process of adding new images and the appropriate dates for each month. To avoid creating too many layers in one document, you may prefer to split the year into two or three documents.

personal stationery

The personal letterhead on page 89 contrasts with the business version on pages 90 and 91. Both versions, however, reflect the character of the people or company they represent.

Although it may be possible to use existing photographs for personal stationery, a more professional result is likely if you shoot the photos with the eventual design in mind. The personal letterhead shown below uses photos of Jane and Michael and their home. The business letterhead is contemporary, with a specially created logo and some graphics added to the background, along with a photo of the proprietor shot in profile.

Creating your own personal or business stationery can have a strong impact on the people with whom you correspond, and doing it yourself will save you lots of money!

CREATING A PERSONAL LETTERHEAD

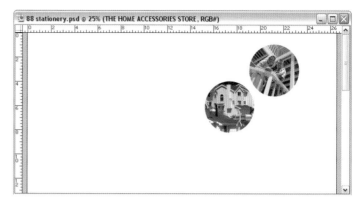

① Open a new letter, 8.5 x 11-in. (A4) document in Photoshop Elements. Paste in the two photos that you are using for the letterhead. Select the *Elliptical Marquee* from the *Tools* palette. Drag it over one of the images until you are satisfied with the crop. Now choose *Inverse* from the *Select* menu and then *Cut* from the *Edit* menu. This will delete the unwanted image area, leaving the remainder within a circular shape.

② Repeat the process with the other photo and then drag each to their desired position at the top right area of the letterhead. Each photo is on a separate layer.

③ Select one photo. From the *Layer Styles* palette, select *Bevels>Simple Inner* and *Drop Shadows>Soft Edge*. This creates a three-dimensional button effect and adds a small round icon to the layer in the *Layers* palette.

④ To fine-tune the bevel and shadow, double-click the icon in the *Layers* palette and make any adjustments that you require. Repeat this process with the other photo.

⑤ On a new layer, select the *Horizontal Type* tool from the *Tools* palette and type in the names. We have used Verdana at 20 point and used the *Eyedropper* tool to select a brown color found in the photos. Add the address details on a new layer and adjust the position of all the elements until they form a satisfactory design.

⑥ The finished letterhead looks professional. The colors are muted, and the address details are simply black and set in 10 point.

CREATING A BUSINESS LETTERHEAD

① Open a new letter-size document in Elements. On a new layer, use the *Rectangular Marquee* tool to draw a rectangle. Use the *Paint Bucket* tool to fill it with a color (here, yellow) to match the photo that you intend to use.

② Deselect the selection. From the *Filters* palette, select *Distort>Wave* from the drop-down menu. Click the *Apply* button. On the next palette, configure the Wave until you are happy with the result in the preview. Keep the two *Scale* sliders to the same value to obtain a result that is balanced on all sides. Then click *OK*. The result should look like this.

③ On a new layer above, paste the photo in a central position about 0.5 in. (1 cm) from the top. Scale it using the *Transform* handles until you are happy with the size.

④ On another new layer, use the *Horizontal Type* tool to enter the company name. Here it is "Fantazia." If you do not have a font like Jokerman, which is the font used here, you could search on the Internet for free fonts. You will soon find hundreds. The color is irrelevant, since we will add a special finish to the logo in a later step.

5 With the text still selected, choose *Create Warped Text* from the *Options* bar. From the *Style* drop-down menu, select *Wave*. Click *OK* to use the default settings.

6 From the *Layer Styles* palette, select *Wow Chrome Beveled Edge* from the *Wow Chrome* drop-down menu. The result is a fantastic 3D chrome effect on the logo.

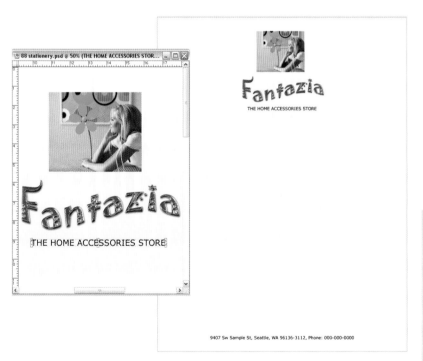

9407 Sw Sample St, Seattle, WA 96136-3112, Phone: 000-000-0000

7 On a new layer, add the subhead in Verdana caps. The size here is 10 point, using black as the color. The final step is to add the address details, centered at the bottom of the page.

→ tip

Folding the letterhead

The main letterhead imagery should be kept within the top third of the page so that when it is folded, it sits comfortably in this area. Place the folded letterhead in an envelope to check that the top third is visible when the envelope flap is torn away.

special print projects

The desktop inkjet printer has become ever more versatile, printing on a wide range of materials in addition to plain paper. Most of the techniques covered in this special print projects section are readily achieved as long as you prepare your digital files properly and follow the printing and finishing directions for each type of printing media. Of course, you may prefer to have a professional printer undertake the printing for you. If so, see the guidelines on page 160.

T-shirts

This project demonstrates how easy it is to print and then transfer an image to a T-shirt or other fabric item.

what you need

- transfer paper
- inkjet printer
- household iron
- scissors
- a flat surface to work on
- a T-shirt

To make this T-shirt, you first print your paper image onto a special transfer paper. This paper is then ironed onto the fabric. Due to the heat involved, you should use a fabric with at least a 50 % cotton content. The transfer process will mirror the image, so the image needs to be flipped horizontally in your image-editing program to maintain the original view. If you prefer to have your T-shirt printed professionally, see the box below.

→ tip

Using a professional printing service

A quick search of the Internet will reveal many custom T-shirt printers that will print single T-shirts or short runs. Printers typically require an image that is less than 2MB in size, usually in JPEG format (*see page 15*). The project on this page is suitable and can easily be converted to JPEG format. You will not need to worry about mirroring the image—your printer will do that for you.

HAPPY BIRTHDAY T-SHIRT

Open a new document in Photoshop Elements; letter, 8.5 x 11-in. (A4) size. Create two new text layers and type in the name and message of your choice. Here the word "Maria" is in red, a color that we will use on the frame later on. The font is Pablo. If you don't have Pablo, substitute a font available on your own computer.

2 Select the *Custom Shape* tool from the *Tools* palette. From the flyout menu, select *Frames* and choose *Frame 19*. Click at the position top left. Holding the cursor down, drag it to the bottom right position of the frame shape. Don't worry if you don't get it right the first time, since you can edit the shape later on.

3 When you draw with the *Custom Shape* tool, a new shape layer is created. To convert this to a regular layer on which you can apply effects, click on the *More>Simplify Layer* button on the *Layers* palette. The *Layer* icon now has a checkerboard background indicating that it is transparent.

4 With the *Shape 1* layer still selected, choose *Wow Plastic>Red* from the *Layer Styles* palette. This effect is now applied to the frame.

5 Paste in the photo to be used within the frame. Use the *Transform* handles to rescale and position it so the area to be shown within the frame is correct.

continued ▶▶

6 Once you are satisfied with the position of the photo, reselect the *Shape 1* layer. Using the *Magic Wand* tool, click in the area outside the frame. Now return to the *Photo* layer and hit the Delete button. This removes the unwanted portion of the photo.

7 Select the topmost layer. From the *Select* menu, choose *All*. Then choose *Copy Merged* from the *Edit* menu. This action makes a copy of all the visible layers, including the background. Again from the *Edit* menu, select *Paste*. The new *Copy Merged* layer is now at the top of the order.

8 From the *Image* menus select *Rotate>Flip Selection Horizontal*. This converts it to the mirror image necessary for the image to appear correctly when it is transferred onto a T-shirt.

9 Steps 7 and 8 can be ignored if your own printer is able to print a mirror image. The option may not be on the *Main* options tab. Follow the transfer paper manufacturers' directions before starting to print. Usually the best quality is the suggested option.

→ tip

Use the template instead

You can download the Tee Shirt.psd document from the web-linked website (see page 166) and simply add your own text and photo.

ironing the printout onto the T-shirt

These directions are for a typical transfer paper, Epson Iron-on Cool Peel Transfer Paper. Other brands may be different, so be sure to read the directions carefully before proceeding. Although transparent, the unprinted background will be apparent where the texture of the fabric has been ironed. If your image is an irregular shape, you may prefer to trim the print back to within a quarter of an inch of it so that the irregularity is less noticeable.

❶ Make sure the T-shirt is free from wrinkles. Place it faceup on a hard, flat surface that is able to withstand heat, such as a sheet of wood or a laminated worktop.

❷ Place the transfer printout facedown on the T-shirt in the position that you want it to appear.

❸ Ensure that the steam setting is turned off. Heat the iron to high/max temperature—usually between 350° and 390°F (180° to 200°C). Cordless irons may not retain heat long enough to complete the process.

❹ Apply steady pressure and heat as you iron over the surface of the printout. This will take between 45 seconds and 1 minute. If you have some spare fabric, it is sensible to do a test transfer with a spare printout.

❺ Leave to cool for a couple of minutes and then carefully peel away the transfer paper, leaving the image imprinted on the garment.

⑩ To convert to JPEG format, select *Save As* from the *File* menu and choose *JPEG* from the drop-down menu. Leave the options as default, which should be *Quality* at 12 Maximum. The resulting file will be about 1.6 MB. If you reduce the quality setting to 6 Medium, the file size will be considerably smaller without much loss of quality.

⑪ A typical online print service has a Browse button to enable you to select the image to be uploaded to the online printer.

refrigerator magnets

Magnetic-backed paper can be used without any special preparation. For most projects, the prints are cut to size after printing, although it is possible to print a full letter-size project if you wish.

We have chosen a 4 x 3-in. (10 x 7.5-cm) size. This enables six items to be printed on a single sheet of paper. Try to put your digital photos to good use in projects like this playground safety reminder and homespun motivational message.

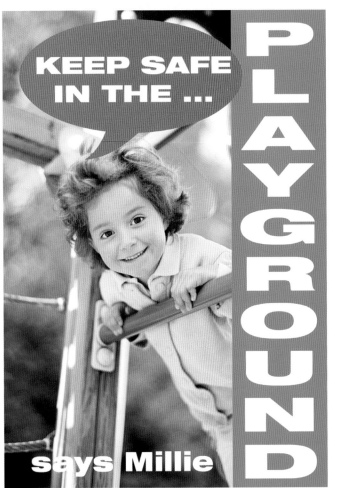

Open a new document in Elements, 4 x 3-in. (10 x 7.5-cm) size. Paste in the photo. In this example, we moved the image to the left, leaving a margin on the right-hand side, since this will be covered by a green panel. On a new layer above the photo, use the *Rectangular Marquee* tool to define a panel. Then sample a color from the image, using the *Eyedropper* tool. Fill the rectangular panel using the *Paint Bucket* tool. We used a green (R 32, G 116, B 38).

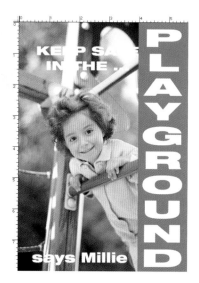

② On a new layer above, use the *Vertical Type* tool to type in the title. We used Helvetica Black Extended at 57 point; you will want to choose a font available on your computer. Use the *Transform* handles to distort the text so that it fits the panel shape. Try to avoid extreme distortion, or the text will be hard to read.

③ On two new layers above, type in the remaining text using the same font as the main title. Don't worry too much about exact positioning since this can be changed later.

④ Select a new foreground color by sampling another color from the photo. For the speech bubble, we chose a red that stands out well against the photo and green panel. Select a *Talk Bubble* from the *Custom Shape* tool options and draw a shape on a new layer below the text but above the panel. This will assume the foreground color that you have just selected. Let the bubble overlap the panel a little. Adjust the text and bubble size until both are correct.

⑤ Chose *All* from the *Select* menu and *Copy Merged* from the *File* menu. Open a new document: letter, 8.5 x 11-in. (A4) size. Paste in the merged image. If you want to duplicate this magnet, paste the image another five times and rearrange the images to fit the page. Alternatively, you could create several magnet projects and paste a variety of images into the new document. Follow the printing directions for the magnetic paper. It is normally the same as regular paper.

permanent decals

For this project, you will need inkjet decal paper on which to print your design. The area for your decal should be flat to avoid creasing when the decal is applied—we've used a plate.

what you need

- inkjet decal paper
- inkjet printer
- lint-free cloth
- dish of water

Although any subject may be suitable for these decals, you may wish to choose something that you are unlikely to tire of—like our dog, Monty, below.

1. Open a new document in Elements. It can be any size as long as it is not smaller than the area of the plate that you intend to fill. We chose 12 x 12 in. (30.5 x 30.5 cm).

2. On a new layer, use the *Elliptical Marquee* tool to define a circle. Choose *Inverse* from the *Select* menu and fill the circle with white using the *Paint Bucket* tool.

3. On a layer below, paste in your photo. Use the *Transform* handles to rescale the image. The image that we chose has an obvious space for the title; your image needs to be carefully chosen with this in mind.

4. Duplicate the layer created in step 2. Use *Adjust Color>Hue/ Saturation* from the *Enhance* menu. Select a color for the image's border. Drag this new layer below the white one. It will temporarily disappear.

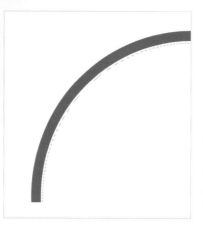

5 With the image still selected, use a corner *Transform* handle to reduce the size of the image. It will now become visible beneath the layer above. Hold down the Shift and Alt keys together while you do this so the image will rescale from its central point.

6 Use the *Magic Wand* tool to make a selection within the circular window. Choose *Inverse* from the *Select* menu. Again from the *Select* menu, choose *Feather*. The actual amount will depend on the size of your image. Between 16 and 64 should be fine.

7 With the selection still active, change to the photo layer and hit the Delete key. This will remove the background of the image, leaving it with a soft (feathered) edge.

8 On two new layers above the others, type in the title and subtitle. We used Caslon semibold small caps and italic; you will want to select fonts available on your computer.

printing and applying the decal

Follow the printing and application directions supplied with the inkjet decal paper; they are likely to be similar to the following:

❶ Make sure the paper is placed in the printer tray correctly, and print with high-quality setting.

❷ Leave the print to dry for a few minutes. Next, in a well-ventilated area, spray with a clear varnish (available from hardware stores). Several coats will be required. Let each dry before applying the next. This is important because the varnish fixes the inkjet printout, which would otherwise run in contact with water.

❸ Cut out the circular image with scissors or a craft knife. Place it in a dish of water for about 30 seconds, or until you can feel the thin membrane slipping away from the backing paper.

❹ Apply some watery glue (diluted white glue) to the area where you are going to place the decal. Then slip off the design from the backing paper and onto the plate. Drain off the water. Smooth out the design with a lint-free cloth to remove the air bubbles. If you want a glossy finish, spray the design with the varnish used earlier.

fabric

An alternative to printing on transfer paper that is then ironed onto fabric is to print directly onto special cotton fabric sheets.

These fabric sheets are letter, 8.5 x 11-in. (A4) size, but you can trim them down to a square. This method would be ideal for a traditional-style quilting project. If prepared properly, the printed fabric should be color fast and washable.

1 Open a new document in Elements, letter, 8.5 x 11-in. (A4) size, and paste in your photo. Use the *Transform* handles to resize it. Trim off the top and bottom to leave a square shape.

2 Select a suitable color for the background of the page. With the *Paint Bucket* tool selected, fill the entire background.

printing and applying the decal

Follow the fabric sheet printing directions supplied with the paper; they are likely to be similar to the following:

❶ The backing sheets must be totally secure before printing. If in doubt, iron them first.

❷ Make sure the paper is placed in the printer tray correctly and the print setting is set to high quality.

❸ Let dry for at least 30 minutes. Then iron for about a minute before peeling off the backing sheet. The fabric is now ready for your project.

3 Switch background and foreground colors, using the icon at the bottom of the *Tools* palette. Select a new foreground color to match a color in the image. Now select the *Brush* tool and pick *Azalea* from the *Special Effect Brushes*.

4 Create a new layer above. Check on the size of the brush from the *Options* bar (we chose 100 pixels). Moving your cursor over the image will reveal the size of the brush. Draw a flowery border around, overlapping the photo. You will see that this *Special Effect Brush* used the foreground and background colors to create a complex floral design.

ALTERNATIVES

The square format does not mean you have to use a square design. This floral border is used to frame a photo that has been trimmed to a circle using the *Elliptical Marquee* tool. Care should be taken, though, to avoid shadows when you shoot the photo of the flowers so they can more easily be cut out from the background.

embossing powder

Embossing powder is used in conjunction with special paper to create a glossy, raised surface to a print. Heat is applied to melt the powder, which then adheres only to the printed area.

Thick embossing paper can withstand heat and is specially treated so the ink doesn't dry instantly. However, be sure to apply the powder immediately after printing. Use a hot-air paint stripper to melt the powder. Do not use a hair dryer because it cannot reach the required temperature.

Open a new document in Elements, letter, 8.5 x 11-in. (A4) size, and paste in your photo. Because the embossing powder adheres to wet ink, images with rich, deep colors that require plenty of ink work best.

Tony Ricardo
Shiraz 04

Tony Ricardo
Shiraz 04

Once you've pasted in your image, you can now add text and a border to complete your design if you choose. Create two new layers and type in the text. We used the font Amazone for the main title and Verdana for the subtitle. You will want to use a font available on your computer.

Tony Ricardo
Shiraz 04

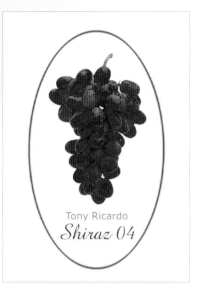

Tony Ricardo
Shiraz 04

3 On a new layer, use the *Elliptical Marquee* tool to define an oval shape surrounding both the photo and text. From the *Select* menu, choose *Modify/Border*. The size will depend on the size of your image. Somewhere between 8 and 19 pixels should be fine.

4 Use the *Paint Bucket* tool to fill the border with a suitable color. We chose a maroon here to match the grapes (R 151, G 27, B 35).

ALTERNATIVES

There are many subjects suitable for embossing. A naturally shiny object such as a car works well with an embossed finish. Of course, you will need to cut it out from the background first.

printing and applying the decal

Follow the embossing paper printing directions supplied with the paper; they are likely to be similar to the following:

1 Be sure to handle the paper only by the edges and away from the image area.

2 Make sure the paper is placed in the printer tray correctly and the print setting is set to high quality.

3 Sprinkle a small amount of embossing powder over the image. Swirl the sheet around to ensure good coverage, and tap the excess onto a spare sheet of paper (it can be reused). Repeat this step if areas of the image do not look sufficiently covered.

4 Use a dry artist's brush to remove any excess powder sticking to the unprinted areas, taking care not to touch the image area.

5 Using a hot-air paint stripper, apply heat to the powdered area. The powder will begin to melt and go clear, leaving a high-gloss raised surface.

adhesive labels

Making a customized jar or bottle label is always a popular project. In this example, we have used an image of a young girl.

The self-assured pose of the child helped to suggest the visual approach and title for the label of this homemade refreshment.

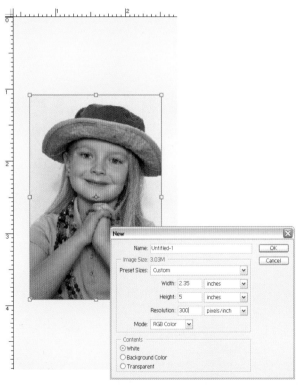

Open a new document in Elements—2.35 x 5-in. (6 x 13-cm) size—and paste in your photo. At this stage, there is no need to rescale the image, since that will be done later. Use the *Paint Bucket* tool to fill the page with a turquoise blue. We used R 195, G 240, B 246.

Miss Emily's
VERY FINE
Peppermint Cordial

Miss Emily's

2 On four new layers, add the text. The typography is important to support the fancy style. Here we have used fonts from the Caslon family. The main title is set in italic with special swash initial caps.

3 When you have positioned the four lines of text, they will occupy the bottom third of the page. The remainder of the page will be used for the photo. Select *Frame 13* from the *Custom Shape* tool options. On a new layer above, define the shape that will surround the photo. It will assume the current foreground color. We chose R 147, G 202, B 210.

ALTERNATIVES
Instead of using an opaque adhesive label, you could use a clear permanent decal (*see page 100*). Using one of these, it's possible to remove the background color and replace it with a thin border so the colored contents of the bottle show through.

4 Use the *Transform* handles to rescale and position the photo so that it appears within the frame. Reselect the frame layer. Using the *Magic Wand,* select the area inside the frame and then choose *Inverse* from the *Select* menu. Reselect the photo layer. With the selection still active, hit the Delete key to remove the unwanted area of the image.

screen projects

It was great to stay for a few days on Debbie and Jack's fabulous boat, a lack of wind stopped us sailing far

Join me on a fabulous journey and visit some of the great places that I have visited during the last three years.

Around the Wor...

Around the World with Gina Dav...

Our Wedding
RACHEL & EDWARD BROWN

Home
Awkward moments
Our little helpers
The Ceremony
The Reception
The Speeches
The Cake

Our Wedding
RACHEL & EDWARD BROWN

Home
Awkward moments
Our little helpers
The Ceremony
The Reception
The Speeches
The Cake

Layers

Multiply | Opacity: 11%

Lock:

Doilly 1
Doilly 2
Doily 3
Frieze
Background

Hi my name is Grace Wilson, I am 32 years old and married to Bob who is 36. Our three children are Will (9), Tom (7) and Tom (5)... and we must ...og called ...just outside ...ly old house ...rden. The boys ...d all things ...e a small ...is a home bird ...s of friends, her ...is painting and

...are quite health ...not obsessive, ...a week and we ...arly. We like to ...ave visited ...stralia where I

...ecorated in ...but we tend to ...we like rather ...for the period look. The garden is a wilderness waiting to be tamed, fortunately Bob's dad Ted is a knowledgeable and

My Favorite Link

Yahoo!
Yahoo! Games
Ya
Ya

N
E

A day at the Zoo

Welcome to my "Day at the Zoo" cyberscrapbook.
My name is Michael Smith, I am eight years old and I love animals.

You don't need to be a design wizard to creatively use your photos on the Web. With just a few simple instructions, you can produce your own albums, galleries, slide shows, and screen savers, as well as e-mail photos to family and friends. For these projects, you need to think in pixels, not inches. If you are unfamiliar with creating pages for the Web, we recommend that you read these project pages sequentially, since each project builds on the skills acquired in the previous one. The websites and source files created for this section can be viewed and downloaded at www.prdpus@web-linked.com.

IN THIS CHAPTER . . .

understanding viewers, players, and browsers

The Web browser is a sort of picture frame in which we view Web pages. That frame includes a range of buttons and menus that can be customized to work best for you. By far the most popular browser, which is built into Windows XP, is MS Internet Explorer. Explorer was also popular on the Mac, but it has been discontinued since Apple introduced its own browser, called Safari.

To enable Web browsers to display video, sound, and animation, there is an additional built-in viewer. In Windows, this is Windows Media Player; on the Mac, it is the QuickTime viewer. In addition to the Web browser, there are other viewers that are needed to view certain types of media. The most popular of these is the Flash Player. This comes preinstalled in all recent browsers. An alternative is Real Player, although this is not usually preinstalled in the browser, and it's now less popular than it once was. All these players are also used as stand-alone applications outside the Web browser. In other words, you can play music, video, and animation from files on your computer rather than from the Web.

You are likely to be prompted to update these browsers and players from time to time. If you don't update them, you'll continue to receive annoying messages like, "To view this page, you must update …" By updating, you'll be able to view ever more sophisticated multimedia entertainment.

In the world of the printed image, an inch is an inch. If you create a letter-size (A4) document and print it on letter-size (A4) paper, you'll get what you expect. A computer's monitor screen is different. The average size is 17 in., but it can be as small as 12 in. or as large as 22 in. Add to this mix the variable resolution of the screen and you begin to see the problem. (Resolution is the number of individual pixels that make up the computer screen image. On a typical 17-in. screen, it is 1,024 pixels across and 768 down.)

Do you know what size your monitor screen is? Well, don't worry—your computer doesn't know either. The computer knows only about resolution. This is still the case even with a notebook computer, where the screen and computer are combined.

INTRODUCING WEB BROWSERS

MENU BAR

ADDRESS BAR

WEB PAGE VIEWING AREA

STATUS BAR

STANDARD BUTTON BAR

LINKS TOOLBAR

✔ Standard Buttons
✔ Address Bar
✔ Links
  Lock the Toolbars
✔ Adobe PDF

▲ This is an Internet Explorer browser window showing the web-linked site from where you can download some of the project files. Right-clicking in the top bar area brings up a dialog box that lets you select which menu bars you want displayed. Make sure that *Lock the Toolbars* is not checked; otherwise, you will not be able to drag the items to a new location.

▲ Safari is supplied with all new Mac OS X computers. It is different in style from Internet Explorer but similar in terms of functionality.

▲ In addition to the Web browser, these are the three main media players: from left to right, Windows Media Player, Flash Player, and QuickTime. When you are viewing Web pages, the player content may be integrated into the browser (like the Flash animation). These screen shots show the players in their stand-alone guise. Windows Media Player is the default player for Windows XP, although it also works on Macs. It will play most movies, music, and sounds. The Flash Player will play only Flash movies/animations. The QuickTime Player is the default on the Mac, although it is also used quite extensively on Windows XP. It, too, is used to read movie, image, and sound files. Many applications can be used to create screen-based projects that can be played by these players.

▲ Real Player, unlike the other players, relies on a specialist content provider who charges for access to material; for that reason, it is generally used by professionals or large corporations.

preparing images for the Web

Photos displayed on the Web need to be made as small as possible (in terms of the size of the file) so that they are quicker to download and view on-screen. However, reducing the file size means taking information out of the photograph, thereby sacrificing quality. The answer is to obtain an optimum balance between file size and image quality—hence, preparing images for the Web is known as optimizing.

One big advantage when viewing images on-screen is that a resolution of 72 ppi (pixels per inch) is perfectly adequate—rather than the 200 or 300 ppi that you need to make good-quality prints. That makes images to be viewed on-screen smaller in terms of file size. As well as thinking in pixels, you have to think in KB (kilobytes). If you think of KB like the weight of this book, for example, the intention of

optimization is to make it lighter without changing its size or appearance. And Photoshop Elements, as well as most other image-editing software, has plenty of tricks to help you do just that (*see pages 114 to 117*).

Before you begin the optimization process, you may need to rescale your photo; in other words, change its dimensions. Follow the steps on page 113 to do this.

see pages 114 to 117

know your equipment

YOUR CAMERA'S QUALITY OPTIONS
If you take photos with the intention of using them for on-screen/Web projects, it may seem expedient to use the lower-quality settings on your camera. This is a mistake; lower quality will usually mean that the images are more compressed. The image sizes will almost certainly have to be changed for screen use and the photograph saved again and recompressed in JPEG format. This means that an unacceptable reduction in image quality is likely.

After you've optimized your images, there are a number of formats in which you can save them. The table (shown left) lists the most common formats for a variety of file types. As you can see, of all of them, JPEG and GIF are by far the most common.

jargon buster
MAIN WEB MEDIA FILE FORMATS

Used for	File Extension
Photographs	.JPG/JPEG (either extension can be used)
Photographs	.PNG-24
Graphics	.GIF
Graphics	.PNG-8
Animation, sound, and video	.SWF (Flash)
Video, sound, and stills	.WMV (Windows Media Player)
Video, sound, and stills	.MOV (QuickTime)
Creating Web pages	.HTM/.HTML

RESIZING AN IMAGE

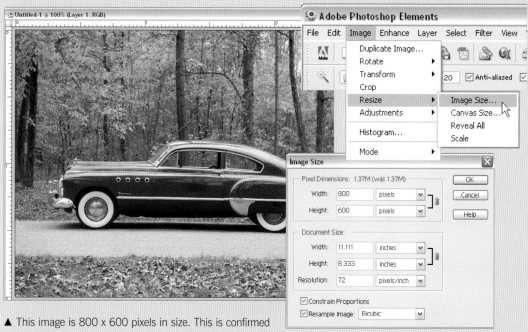

▲ This image is 800 x 600 pixels in size. This is confirmed by selecting *Resize>Image Size* from the *Image* drop-down menu. The dialog box also indicates that the image is 72 ppi.

▲ To resize the image, return to the *Image Size* palette and alter *Width* to between 400 and 600 pixels. Ensure that the *Constrain Proportions* option is checked, and the *Height* will automatically change as well. The *Resample Image* option should also be checked to enforce the change. The car photo is now reduced to the new size.

OPTIMIZING AN IMAGE

FILE FORMAT

IMAGE QUALITY

ORIGINAL IMAGE SIZE

NEW IMAGE SIZE

DOWNLOAD TIME MEASURED IN SECONDS: IT VARIES ACCORDING TO THE SPEED OF THE LINK

PREVIEW YOUR IMAGE IN THE BROWSER OF YOUR CHOICE

▲ After you've changed the image dimensions, select *Save for Web* under the *File* menu. This dialog box provides you with everything you need to optimize an image for the Web. Here we've optimized a photo using the JPEG format. This is the most popular option, particularly for photos, since it has a wide range of quality settings. Here the preview, zoomed to 400%, shows

minimal loss at a *Quality* level set to Medium 50. The file size has been dramatically reduced to 62 KB from 703 KB, which gives an average download time of 12 seconds with a 56 K modem. Experiment with the *Quality* slider until you reach an acceptable balance between image quality and image size. The *Progressive* box, if ticked, enables the image to display a bit at a time.

◄ PNG-24 format is less popular because it doesn't have variable quality options. This means that the file sizes are inevitably larger, like this one at 465 KB. PNG-24, like JPEG, does not need to reduce the number of colors in the original. They can both use more than 16 million different colors.

▲ GIF is another popular format. It is used mainly for Web graphics (as opposed to photographs). The colors in the original image are reduced to a maximum of 256. This results in blockiness, especially when the available colors are reduced to just 32, as shown here. As the Photoshop Elements' tip box says at the top of the screen, *Save photographs as JPEG and images with limited colors as GIF*.

► GIF comes into its own with text and images that have effects like *Posterize* applied to them. The preview window shows the optimized image before it is saved, but if you hit the *Preview In...* button, you can see the result in the browser.

continued ▶▶

▲ GIF can also be saved with a transparent background, enabling an image in the background to show through. Here the number of colors has been reduced to just 4, enabling the file size to be reduced to 10 KB. The ability to support a transparent background is also true of PNG.

◄ Although PNG-24 creates files that are larger than JPEG, it does have one significant advantage—it enables background transparency in a photographic quality image (remember that it uses 16 million colors).

WMV is a format that is used when you create a Photo Story using Microsoft Plus Digital Media Edition. This application generates a sophisticated slide show without requiring the user to have any previous skills in this area. There are two quality options when you save the file: High and Medium.

▲ WMV is also the format used to output a movie created using Microsoft MovieMaker. The application is used primarily for creating movies on your computer but can also be used very effectively to display still images.

▲ On the Mac OS X computer, iMovie is the popular alternative to MS MovieMaker. Its files are saved in QuickTime format. In addition, iPhoto is used to manage, enhance, and store digital photographs.

Save an image to include in a Web page.
Save photographs as JPEG and images with limited colors as GIF
The image preview shows how your image will look using the current settings.

OK

Cancel

Help

Settings: Custom
JPEG
Maximum
Progressive
ICC Profile
Optimize
Quality: 84
Matte:

e-mailing your photos

Sending your digital photos by e-mail offers a quick and easy way to share photos with family and friends. Do keep in mind, though, that the e-mail recipient usually has no way of stopping an e-mail downloading to his or her computer. So think about the size of the attachments before sending.

To keep your attachments small, make sure the attached image has been optimized to the smallest possible file size (*see pages 112–117*). Many people do not have a broadband (fast) connection, and it is very irritating to see your e-mail software endlessly awaiting an incoming message. When sending an e-mail, always type a descriptive phrase in the message subject box. If you do decide to send an unsolicited e-mail and it is to multiple locations (a Christmas card, for example), use the BCC (blind carbon copies) option to hide other recipients' e-mail addresses.

E-MAIL PHOTO MESSAGE

Open a new document 500 x 350 pixels with *Resolution* set to 72 pixels/inch as shown above.

Paste in the photo and use the *Transform* handles to rescale to fit the area required.

3 Select the background and use the *Paint Bucket* tool to fill with a color of your choice. Here, we have matched the rim of Jim's cap.

4 On a new layer above the others, select the *Horizontal Type* tool and type in the headline. We have used a funky font called Pompeia. Repeat this process, this time with the main message; you will probably want to use a smaller font size than that used for the headline.

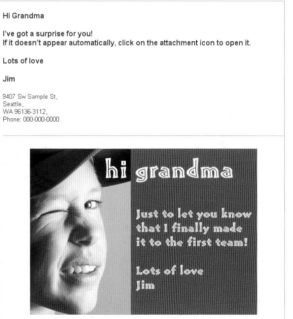

5 From the *File* menu, select *Save for Web* and choose *JPEG*. We left the settings as default except for *Quality*. A level of 84 was necessary to avoid degrading the text, but the resulting file size was still below 72 KB.

6 Now the JPEG file has been optimized, and it's ready to attach to an e-mail message. Here Jim is e-mailing his grandmother with some special news that is contained in the image created in steps 1 to 5. He is using MS Outlook Express and has personalized the background selecting *Maize* from the *Format>Apply Stationery* menu.

creating your own online photo gallery

Using Photoshop Elements to create a Web gallery that can be shared online or put onto a CD is easy. Simply follow the steps described in the next few pages, and within minutes you could be sharing your latest vacation photos with relatives on the other side of the world.

Now that you've discovered how to optimize images for the Web, you're ready to create an online photo gallery that anyone can view on the Internet. You could also copy your gallery to a CD to give to a friend or family member to enjoy. The number of images you can put in your gallery is almost limitless, allowing you to add additional photos at any time. A gallery is a perfect way to show and share your family's latest happenings.

CREATING THE GALLERY

→ tip

Naming your files

During the course of this project, you will be asked to name the photo files as you save them. Remember to give the photos descriptive names, since these will be how the photos are labeled when they appear in the gallery. However, there are strict limitations for pages that are to be transferred to a Web server: Commas and spaces between words are not allowed—an underscore must be used instead. For example: familyvacation_florida2004

1 Create a folder called "Web Photo Gallery." Within that folder, create another folder called "Originals." Drag the images that you plan to use into this folder. Open each image in Photoshop Elements and select *Save for Web* from the *File* menu. Choose *JPEG* as the file type and select a *Quality* value that is suited to your image. Here, it is 40. In the *New Size* option, type in 500 (pixels) as the *Width* value. Ensure that *Constrain Proportions* is checked. Then hit the *Apply* button. If the photo is portrait format, change the *Height* to 500 (pixels) instead.

2 Click *OK* at the end of step 1 and name each file using a short descriptive phrase of no more than 30 letters and spaces. Do not use characters other than letters or numbers. The file name will be used as the title for each photo in the gallery. To ensure that the photos display in the desired order, add a number at the beginning of each file name.

3 Select *Web Photo Gallery* from the *File* menu. The resulting palette has a range of options. Select your preferred option from *Styles*. We chose *Lace*. Click the *Browse* button and select *Originals*, the folder that contains your photos. Click the *Destination* button and select the *Web Photo Gallery* folder. From the *Options* menu, select *Banner* and type in the site name. All other settings can be left at the default values. Click *OK*. Elements takes 20–30 seconds to create the Web gallery and launch it in the browser.

4 The home page has a series of thumbnail images that, when clicked, fire up the relevant page with the full-size (500-pixel) image. Navigational arrows enable you to toggle through the images without returning to the home page.

5 The folder that you created and called "Originals" has now been joined by three other folders and two files called "index" and "UserSelections." These are automatically created by Elements. Double-clicking on the index file will fire up the home page in the browser.

using online photo gallery services

Online services are easy to use, particularly when putting photos on the Internet. In just minutes, your relatives and friends can see your photos.

Most camera manufacturers offer this service, and it's usually free, so you can expect to be offered additional paid-for services as well. It is usually best to prepare the images that you wish to use in advance—for example, removal of red-eye, improving contrast, and so on *(see pages 28–37)*. Most online galleries will have an image file size or maximum image-dimension limitation.

Kodak Ofoto (www.ofoto.com) is an online photo gallery that includes a free assemble-and-upload utility called OfotoNow. This utility can be downloaded and installed on your computer. Your photos can then be uploaded to an online Ofoto album and e-mails with the relevant link sent to you. Your photos can also be saved as a screen saver, but only on the user's computer. Ofoto is closely associated with Kodak Easyshare.

Sony ImageStation (found at www.imagestation.com) is another online gallery. This is an online photo album with a variety of themes and backgrounds that can be selected to enhance your photos. You can easily upload your images by dragging-and-dropping and you can even add simple captions.

Both online galleries require registration before you can start uploading. Once you see the photos in the browser, you know that you are looking at them on the website and not on your own computer.

USING SONY IMAGESTATION

To use ImageStation, first connect to the website. You will need to fill in the joining forms if it is your first visit. To upload images from your computer, select the folder that contains the photos that you wish to upload. Simply drag them onto the blue target on the ImageStation browser window and then click the *Upload* button. (When you drag and drop onto the target, you are not moving the original image, just a copy of it.)

Wait for the upload to complete. There will be an upload confirmation. Next, click the *Go to Storage Bin* button, where you will see the images. Click the *Create New Album* button. You will be prompted to fill in some details. Click *Continue*. You will then be prompted to choose an Album Style.

The style applied here is *Travel>Mass Transit*. Next, click *Enter* to view your album.

You can edit each image online and apply enhancements using the *Effects*, *Textures*, *Templates*, or *Edges* buttons.

USING KODAK OFOTO

To use the Ofoto service, log onto the website and fill in the membership form. To upload images, click the *Ofoto* icon to launch the application and select *Get Photos*. Click the tick boxes to select the photos you wish to use. You have the option to rename photos. This alters the file name on your computer, so it is sensible to make a duplicate backup of the folder.

Click the *Upload* button and insert your e-mail address and password.

You will be prompted to fill in details for your new album. When you have completed these, click the *Finish* button. The upload process will begin automatically.

When the uploading is complete, your photos will appear in the browser window. On the right-hand side, various options are displayed that enable you to add titles to each photo as well as other enhancements.

5 Choose a border or other effect. Here, the softened edge (vignette) was selected from the *Borders>Studio* sub-menu. This is immediately applied to your photo. You will have to apply this effect individually to each photo, using the arrow buttons to move from image to image.

6 Next, select each photo in turn and click *Add Photo Title*. Add your preferred title in the pop-up window.

7 Your online album is now complete. Thumbnails of your photos appear in a new window. Click on the *Slideshow* link, and they will appear full-size.

8 Finally, click on the *Share Photos* tab if you wish family or friends to see your new online album. You will be prompted to fill in their e-mail addresses along with a message.

setting up a home page

Both professionally and personally, a home page gives you the opportunity to share your world. You can personalize it with photos and a variety of links to other sites. The possibilities are endless.

There are two ways to create websites. One method is to master complex Web-authoring software; the other, much simpler method is to use an online page builder like Yahoo! GeoCities. This allows PageWizards to create simple Web pages based on existing templates, and some of the space is free. To make the process easier, a little preparation will help. For example, resize and optimize your images, or you will quickly run out of the free space that Yahoo! GeoCities offers.

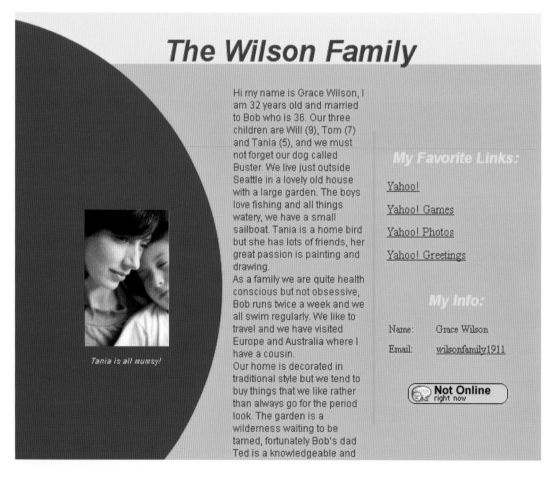

The Wilson Family

Hi my name is Grace Wilson, I am 32 years old and married to Bob who is 36. Our three children are Will (9), Tom (7) and Tania (5), and we must not forget our dog called Buster. We live just outside Seattle in a lovely old house with a large garden. The boys love fishing and all things watery, we have a small sailboat. Tania is a home bird but she has lots of friends, her great passion is painting and drawing.

As a family we are quite health conscious but not obsessive, Bob runs twice a week and we all swim regularly. We like to travel and we have visited Europe and Australia where I have a cousin.

Our home is decorated in traditional style but we tend to buy things that we like rather than always go for the period look. The garden is a wilderness waiting to be tamed, fortunately Bob's dad Ted is a knowledgeable and

Tania is all mumsy!

My Favorite Links:

Yahoo!

Yahoo! Games

Yahoo! Photos

Yahoo! Greetings

My Info:

Name: Grace Wilson

Email: wilsonfamily1911

Not Online right now

USING YAHOO! GEOCITIES

→ tip

The Yahoo! ID

When you apply for a Yahoo! ID, this becomes
your log-in name and part of your website URL:
(http://www.geocities.com/name_placeholder).
The demonstrations on this and the following pages
have "name_placeholder" wherever the log-in name
you have chosen will appear.

Hi my name is Grace Wilson, I am
32 years old and married to Bob
who is 36. Our three children are
Will (9), Tom (7) and Tania (5),
and we must not forget our dog
called Buster. We live just outside
Seattle in a lovely old house with a
large garden. The boys love fishing
and all things watery, we have a
small sailboat. Tania is a home bird
but she has lots of friends, her
great passion is painting and
drawing.

As a family we are quite health
conscious but not obsessive, Bob
runs twice a week and we all swim
regularly. We like to travel and we
have visited Europe and Australia
where I have a cousin.

Our home is decorated in
traditional style but we tend to buy
things that we like rather than
always go for the period look. The
garden is a wilderness waiting to
be tamed, fortunately Bob's dad
Ted is a knowledgeable and willing
helper and we are hoping to finish
the major paving and planting later
this year.

This is our first web page and so I
hope it works ok
Grace Wilson

1 To save time later, when you are online, first type your
text into a word processor and then choose a portrait-
format photo to accompany it. Resize the photo so that it is
400 pixels deep and optimize it *(see page 112–117)*.

2 Connect to the Internet and then to the Yahoo!
GeoCities sign-up page. You must complete a form with
your details before proceeding. Because this service is free,
banner ads may be included on your page.

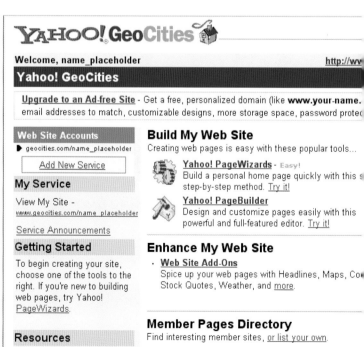

3 From *Build My Web Site*, select *Yahoo! PageWizards*.

continued ►►

USING YAHOO! PAGEWIZARDS

Welcome, name_placeholder

http://www.geocities.com/name_placeholder

geocities.com/name_placeholder   **GeoCities Free**

Home > **PageWizards**

✿ Yahoo! PageWizards

PageWizards are a fun and fast way to make cool web pages. Just answer a few questions and build a professional-looking web page in minutes.

Quick Start - Eight designs to choose from and just four easy steps.

Fun D'Mental   Techie   Night Vision   Disk Drive

Get Yahoo! SiteWizards

Build a multi-page site in minutes - no coding required! Move up to a Yahoo! Web Hosting plan.

Setup Fee Waived!
Limited time offer

Featured Themes
Photo Page

 Include a message and up to eight photos with captions. Choose from eight designs.

 From the *Eight Quick Start* designs, select *Fun D'Mental*.

⑤ The Welcome screen introduces the four steps of the process. Click the *Begin* button.

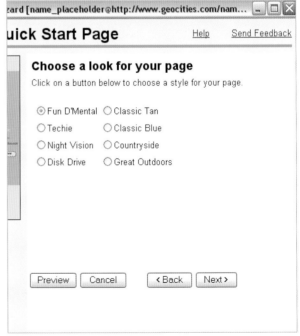

⑥ If you want to change the design, select an alternative and click the *Preview* button. Then click the *Next* button.

7 Enter the title and then either type in the text or paste in the text that you prepared earlier. Click the *Next* button.

8 Click the *Upload new image* button so that you can select the photo to accompany the text.

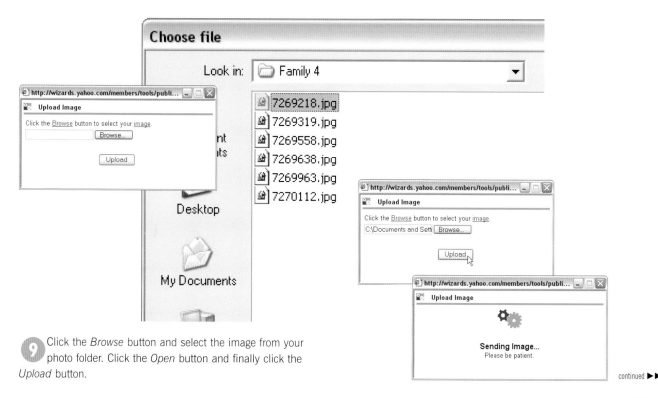

9 Click the *Browse* button and select the image from your photo folder. Click the *Open* button and finally click the *Upload* button.

continued ▶▶

USING YAHOO! PAGEWIZARDS–CONTINUED

❸ Enter your favorite links

Type in your favorite links. Visitors to your page will then be able to go to these pages. Below are some suggested links. You can change or delete these.

Name your favorite links section:

My Favorite Links:

	Link Name (ex. My favorite page)	Web Address (ex. www.yahoo.com)
1.	Yahoo!	www.yahoo.com
2.	Yahoo! Games	games.yahoo.com
3.	Yahoo! Photos	photos.yahoo.com
4.	Yahoo! Greetings	greetings.yahoo.com

❹ Enter your information

Name your personal info section:

My Info:

Your name:

Grace Wilson

Your email address:

name_placeholder

(ex. yourname@yahoo.com)

Let people know when you are online. If you have Yahoo! Messenger, this indicator will let visitors send you an instant message.

☑ Put this on my page

⑩ The resulting Links page enables you to add some personal links. For the time being, we will leave the default settings. Click the *Next* button.

⑪ Add your personal information. If you want to use the message service, leave the *I'm Online* button checked. Click the *Next* button.

uick Start Page   Help   Send Feedback

Name your page

Type in a name for your page or use the one suggested below. This name will be part of your page's web address, which will be used when your friends view your page.

Page name: index

(example: **My_page** or **mypage**)

uick Start Page   Help   Send Feedback

Congratulations!

You have finished creating your own Quick Start Page. You and your friends can now view your page at the web address below!

Please write down your web address for future reference.

http://www.geocities.com/name_placeholder/
The_Wilson_Family.html

⑫ Use "index" as the name for your page. This is important: The home page on all websites must always be named "index." You can give any additional pages a descriptive name. Remember to use an underscore instead of a space between words. Click the *Next* button.

⑬ PageWizards has now been completed. Your Yahoo! ID—the name that you used to sign on to the Yahoo! GeoCities service—will appear instead of "name_placeholder" in your Web address. Click the *Done* button.

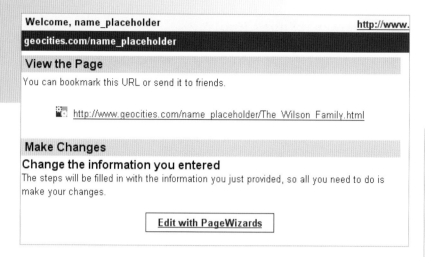

Welcome, name_placeholder   **http://www.**
geocities.com/name_placeholder

View the Page

You can bookmark this URL or send it to friends.

 http://www.geocities.com/name_placeholder/The_Wilson_Family.html

Make Changes

Change the information you entered

The steps will be filled in with the information you just provided, so all you need to do is make your changes.

Edit with PageWizards

14 You can now either view your page or make changes to it using the *Edit with PageWizards* button (*see step 15*). The next project (*see pages 132–135*) shows how you can enhance your page with another application called PageBuilder.

→ **tip**

The Yahoo! GeoCities free service

At the time of writing, the steps shown on this page are correct. If Yahoo! GeoCities makes any alterations or improvements, a revised page will be published on the web-linked.com website, which all purchasers of this book have access to *(see page 166)*.

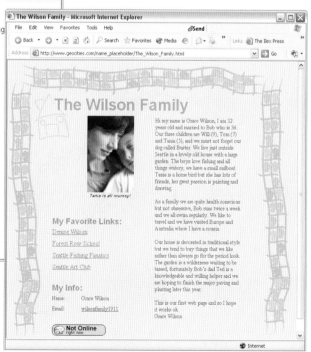

15 If you want, you can edit your Web page at any time. In this example, we have selected the *Countryside* design and personalized the *My Favorite Links* section. Clicking the *Preview* button displays the revised page in the browser.

designing a personal website

The next stage is to design a website. By using an online tool known as Yahoo! PageBuilder, this is simple to do.

PageBuilder enables you to design your own website using simple, intuitive tools. You can start with one of the templates provided and then adapt and personalize it if you wish, adding new photos and text. To use this service, you need to be connected to the Internet. To obtain a Yahoo! ID, see the box on page 127.

USING PAGEBUILDER

Begin the design of your website by first connecting to the Internet. Open the Yahoo! GeoCities Web page and sign in. (This may not be necessary; the website will probably recognize you if you have signed in previously.) Click on the *Countryside* design using the *Quick Start* template option. A small browser window will open. This is the "engine" that drives PageBuilder. It must not be closed until you have finished working on your site.

→ **tip**

First, optimize your photos

Although PageBuilder will let you resize your photos while you are designing your pages, it is best to prepare them for Web use first. A convenient size is 400 pixels wide or deep, whichever is the longest. Each image should then be optimized using Photoshop Elements or a similar image-editing application (*see pages 114–117*).

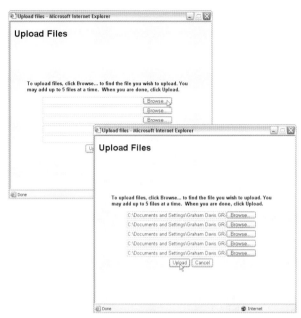

2 The resulting page will show the "Countryside" image as a background to the page, along with blue rectangles containing text and one with an image (a flower graphic). Double-click on the graphic, and the *Select Picture* palette will appear. The *Picture List* shows the default images. Since we want to add our own image, hit the *Upload* button.

3 The *Upload Files* window appears with five *Browse* buttons. Click on a *Browse* button. From the *Choose File* window, select the folder containing the images that you want to use for your Web pages. Choose one of these and click *Open*. Repeat the process until all five *Upload* options contain an image, then click the *Upload* button. Another window will appear to confirm the successful upload.

4 Double-click on the flower graphic again. From the *Picture List* menus, double-click on the *Parent Directory* and again on *User Files*. The files that you have just uploaded will appear on the list. Select the photo to be used on the home page and hit the *OK* button. Your own image will now replace the flower graphic. If you have selected the wrong image, simply double-click on it and select another. As the new photo is bigger than the flower graphic, it overlaps some of the text. This is indicated by the red cross-hatching.

5 Using the corner handle, make the image fit within the column. Don't worry that some of the overlap persists; we will return to that later.

continued ▶▶

6 We now turn our attention to the text. For technical reasons, it is not possible to paste text into the PageBuilder text blocks, so it has to be typed in. Start with the title, the update message, and the main text.

7 Click on the photo and drag it off to the right. Delete the text blocks that were overlapped by it, then move it back to the previous position. The red cross-hatching will have disappeared.

8 Select each of the remaining three website links (below the photo) and type in your alternatives. With text selected, click on the *Links* button. From the resulting *Hot Links* palette, with the *Web URL* option selected, type in a Web address to match the name. If you wish to add your own e-mail address to *My Info use*, follow the same process but make sure *E-Mail* is selected and not *Web URL*.

9 With the title selected, click on the *Choose Text Color* button and select a new color. You can change the color of all text blocks if you wish.

You have now finished adapting the page. It is time to see what it looks like in the browser. Click the *Preview* button and the page will appear.

If you are happy with the result, select *Save* from the *File* drop-down menu. Since this is the website's home page, it must be called "index"—you don't have any choice!

adding another page to your website

❶ To add another page to your website, repeat step 1 from page 132. A new page will appear using the same *Countryside* background. Since we want this page to contain only photos and captions, delete all the other text blocks. Leave just the flower graphic, caption, and the title, which we have changed to "Dad's Cooking."

❷ Double-click on the flower graphic. From the *Select Picture* palette, choose the first image (as in step 4). Resize the image to a convenient size and type in a real caption below it. Click the *Pictures* button. Select the next image from the *User Files* menu and resize this also. Continue adding and resizing photos until complete. Now turn your attention to the remaining captions. The easiest way is to click on the existing caption and then, from the *Edit* menu, select *Duplicate*. Drag the duplicate caption to the new position and type over with the correct text.

❸ The second page is now complete, except that a link is needed back to the home page. Clicking the *Text* button creates a new empty text block. Use the handles to make this a convenient size and then drag it to a new location at the top of the page. Type in "Home Page" and, with the text selected, click on the *Links* button. Select *My Page* from the *Link to a Location* drop-down menu and select *index.html*.

❹ From the *File* menu, select *Save* and name the page. Remember to use an underscore (_) instead of a space between words.

❺ Click on the *Open* button and select index (the home page). We now need to add a link from here to the "Dad's Cooking" page that we have just created. Repeat step 3 and save the page. Next you will see a window stating *Save and Publish is complete*. These pages can now be viewed by anyone on the Internet.

making a cyberscrapbook

Many of you probably have enjoyed creating scrapbooks with pictures and words that detail a family event. Here we show you how to make a cyberscrapbook.

To make a cyperscrapbook (a scrapbook that can be viewed on the Internet), we are going to create our own background and navigation buttons instead of those supplied by PageBuilder. The Web graphics and photos are prepared using Photoshop Elements. These are then uploaded and the Web pages created using Yahoo! GeoCities PageBuilder.

DESIGNING THE BACKGROUND

A day at the Zoo

There are so many different types of animal at the zoo. The antelope is very nervous except when he can't see you; the hippo is so relaxed he doesn't mind having a little bird on his head.

Open a new document in Photoshop Elements, 1,000 x 630 pixels. This will be used to assemble the various items to be used on the website. On a new layer, use the *Lasso* tool from the *Tools* palette to draw a freehand line (simulating a torn edge) roughly 100 pixels from the left side. Continue it along the bottom, side, and top until you join up with the start point. Release the mouse, and you will have completed the shape.

2 Use the *Paint Bucket* tool to fill the shape with color. We used R 71, G 207, B 180. Using the *Rectangular Marquee* tool, define a rectangle, the left side of which is aligned with 680 pixels on the *Ruler*. Fill this with the same color. This will be used as a background image on the Web page. As it will repeat, the bottom of the image needs to join up with the top. A quick way of ensuring this is to use the *Rectangular Marquee* tool to define a small rectangle about 20 pixels deep. Align it to the right of an imagined vertical line at the 100-pixel point. We have zoomed in so it is visible. Now delete the small area of image within the marquee. Repeat this at the bottom of the page.

3 From the *Layer Styles* palette, select the *Soft Edge* drop shadow. After it has been applied, double-click the *Layer Styles* icon on the *Layers* palette. Change the *Lighting Angle* to 180°. This causes the shadow to appear horizontally rather than obliquely. If left at the default setting, a gap will be apparent if the background image repeats.

continued ▶▶

From the *Tools* palette, change the foreground color to a darker shade. We chose R 51, G 153, B 128. Click on the *Rectangle* tool flyout menu and select the *Custom Shape* tool. Now choose the *Paw Print* from the *Options* bar. Use the cursor to drag out the paw shape. This automatically creates a new layer, Shape 1. From the *More* button on the *Layers* palette, select *Simplify Layer*. This converts it into a normal editable layer.

Position the paw-print image. Then duplicate the layer twice to create the other two images. On a new layer beneath each paw layer, use the *Horizontal Type* tool to add the text "Page 1," "Page 2," and "Page 3." We used 10-point Arial bold in the same color as the paw graphic.

On a new layer, type in the title; we used a font called Spumoni at 80-point size. The layers created so far should look like this. If you want to change any of the layer names, you can do so by double-clicking on them.

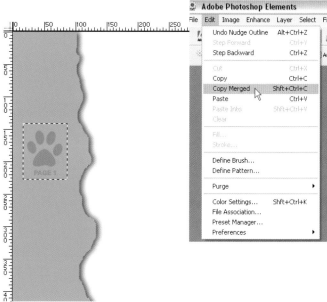

7 Turn off all the layers except the green edge. From the File menu, select *Save for Web*. Select *GIF* and change the colors to 16. Leave the other settings as default and click *OK*. We called the file "green edge background."

8 To save the buttons for Web use, use the *Rectangular Marquee* tool to make a selection around one. Now select *Edit>Copy Merged*. This copies all layers so you can paste them into a new document as a combined layer.

9 Select *File>New* and then *OK*. Select *Edit>Paste,* and the button image appears. From the *File* menu, select *Save for Web*. Select *GIF* and change the colors to 8. Leave the other settings as default and click *OK*. We called the file "button_page_1." Repeat this with the other buttons.

10 Now make a selection around the title and repeat the process described previously. You now have five GIF files that will be used as your website interface. Reducing the number of colors in a GIF file can produce tiny file sizes. The buttons are only 1KB each.

continued ▶▶

Connect to the Internet and sign in to Yahoo! Geocities PageBuilder, as described in the previous project. When the PageBuilder page displays, select *FileManager* from the *File* menu.

The PageBuilder FileManager shows the pages that you have created and files that you have uploaded, as well as those that PageBuilder supplies to all users. For the moment, it is empty. Select the *Images* tab and hit the *Upload* button. We will begin the process of transferring the GIF files created previously.

From the *Upload Files* palette, click the *Browse* button and select a GIF file. Click *Open* (a rather confusing button name, since the file does not open!), and repeat the process until all five files have been selected. When the upload is complete, FileManager displays all the five images. If you need to delete one at any time, check the relevant *Select* box.

Return to the PageBuilder window and select *Basic > Background* from the *Insert* menu. In the *Picture List,* click on the Parent Directory to access your files saved under User Files. Choose the background image. A small preview picture will appear. Click *OK* (not *Upload*, as we have already completed this stage).

ASSEMBLING PAGE CONTENT

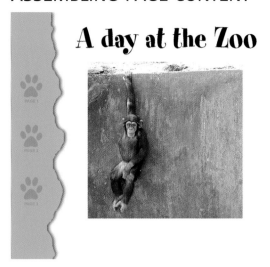

15 The background image now appears on the page. Click the *Picture* button and select *button 1*. Click *OK,* and it will appear on your page. Repeat this process with the other two buttons and drag each of them to the correct position.

17 We have finished with PageBuilder for the moment and now return to Elements. Even though individual images have to be saved for Web use, it is often convenient to assemble the elements in one layered file, as we are doing. It enables the designer to balance size, proportion, and color in a way that would be much more difficult if the elements were all created separately. Paste in the photo of the chimp that will be used on the home page. It is larger than the total page size, so zoom out to a convenient size (probably 25%) and use the *Transform* handles to reduce it to the desired size.

16 Repeat the process again with the title. You can reposition the images at any time by simply dragging them. Remember that with the exception of the background image, no other images (or text) should overlap.

18 Paste in the photo of our young website author above the chimp layer and resize to overlap the chimp at bottom right. From the *Layer Styles* menu, select *Drop Shadow>Soft Edge*. If the Lighting Angle is still 180°, uncheck *Global Light* and change it back to 120° (the default setting). With *Global Light* checked, changing the lighting angle will make all previously applied drop shadows change too. Use the *Rectangular Marquee* tool to make a selection around the two photos. Select *File>New*. Then click *OK* and *Paste* from the *Edit* menu and the image appears.

continued ▶▶

19 From the *File* menu, select *Save for Web*. These photos need to be saved in JPEG. Leave the settings at default except for *Quality*. This can be reduced to 40, resulting (coincidentally) in a file size of just over 40KB. This is large, but not excessively so. Check *Progressive*. This enables the image to display gradually—useful over slow Internet connections.

21 Connect to the Internet and sign in again to Yahoo! GeoCities PageBuilder. Your home page should open by default. Repeat the file uploading process described in steps 12 to 14, this time with the three new JPEG images. Use the *Pictures* button to select the chimp photo to be used on the home page. When it appears, drag it to the correct position.

20 Repeat the process described in the previous three steps for the images to be used on the other two pages. We can now dispense with Elements for the remainder of the project.

22 The home page is now nearly complete. It will be used to form the basis of the other two pages. Make sure you save it first. Then, from the *File* menu, select *Save As* and call it page 2. Repeat the process with page 3. From the *File* menu, select *FileManager*. You will see the three pages if you click on the *Pages* tab.

23 The final task is to add page links to the buttons and add some text to each page. Return to index, the home page, and click on the *Page 2* button to select it. Click on the *PageBuilder Link* button. From the *Hot Link* palette, select the *My Page* option. Now choose *page 2* and click *OK*. Repeat this process with the *Page 3* button. Since we will be editing the home page, it does not need a link to itself, so don't create a link for the *Page 1* button.

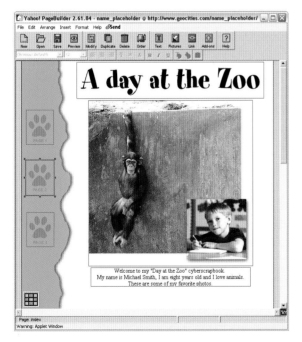

24 Click on the *Text* button. Drag the resulting text box to a position under the photo. It can be made wider or deeper to fit the text using the cursor. Select the centered text icon from the *Options* bar and type in the text. The home page is now complete. After saving this page, open page 2 and add links and text to it. Repeat this process for page 3.

25 The finished pages can be checked in the browser to see if the links have been added correctly.

→ tip

The background image

If your computer screen is large enough, you will be able to see how the background image repeats itself (this is called "tiling") when your browser is maximized. Since we made the image 1,000 pixels wide, it is unlikely to repeat on the width. However, if your text block were 20 lines instead of just 3, a scroll bar would appear on your browser. When you scroll down to the bottom, the effect of tiling would become apparent.

creating an online wedding album

One of life's most memorable events can now be recreated and shared through an online album using PageBuilder—and perhaps even a little lace.

The PageBuilder page defaults constrain the page width to 650 pixels and prohibit images from overlapping. We have changed the default settings for this project to allow for overlay. A text list of links to other pages has been added to each page to enable navigation. Our design is contemporary and complements the informality of the photos.

CREATING THE BACKGROUND

THE LACE PAPER DOILY IMAGE

We scanned a lace paper doily and used it as an integral part of the design. If yours is white, you will need to scan it against a black background. After scanning, select *Image> Adjustments>Invert*. The image is now black on white. If the scan is a bit gray, boost the contrast using *Enhance> Adjust>Brightness*. Use the *Magic Wand* to make a selection outside the lace paper. Delete this area. Use the *Magic Wand* again on the black area of the doily and delete that. You will be left with a white image of what was originally cut out.

Open a new document in Photoshop Elements, 1,000 x 630 pixels. This will be used to assemble the various items to be used on the website. Use the *Paint Bucket* tool to fill the background with color. We used R 196, G 181, B 229. Paste the lace paper doily image (see box at left) on a new layer and reduce the *Opacity* to between 45% and 15%. Repeat this process twice more.

On a new layer below the lace doilies, add the frieze image across the top. Then change the *Layer Blend Mode* to *Multiply* and reduce *Opacity* to 11%. This lets the background show through the image.

As we want the title to appear on every page, we are making it part of the background image. We have used two fonts: Ribbon (120 point) for "Our Wedding" and Birch (42 point) for the names.

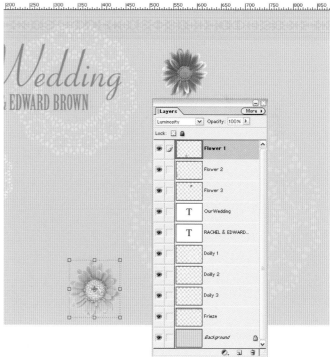

The three flower images that we have already cut out (see box below) are pasted into new layers above the others. Rescale them if necessary and position as required.

THE FLOWER IMAGES

The flower images need to be cut out. After scanning the flowers, open the image file. Next, use the *Lasso Tool* to define a shape around the flower. Then go to *Select> Inverse>Delete*. Use the *Magic Wand* to select an area and delete that. Carry on until you are left with the awkward areas; use the *Selection Brush* to remove these.

Using the *Layers* palette, change the *Layer Blend Mode* of the three flower layers to *Luminosity*. They will now adopt the color of the layer below. Reduce *Opacity* as well if necessary.

continued ▶▶

6 On a new layer above the others, paste in the main image to be used on the home page. Use the *Transform* handles to rescale them. Zoom out to 25% or whatever is necessary to see the extent of the image. The size of this image will be the basis for photos to be used on other pages.

7 Create a new document to enable you to choose which photos you want to go on the website. Open a new document, 1,500 x 1,200 pixels. Copy the photo used in step 6 and paste it into the top left of the page. Paste in the photos that you intend to use for the first few Web pages. Rescale them and then select *Layers>More>Merge Visible*. Ensure that the background is turned off before doing so. Using the same background color as the main document will help if you need to enhance any of the photos.

SAVING IMAGES FOR WEB USE

8 For the moment, return to the main document and turn off the photo so that just the background graphics remain visible (as the image in step 5). From the *File* menu, select *Save for Web*. Use the *Hand* tool to drag the area previewed, as shown in the screen shot. This shows all the elements of the image—text, frieze, flower, and lace doily. This is important, since the number of colors must be reduced to the absolute minimum when saving a GIF in order to reduce the file size. Here, we have reduced the number to 12 while retaining acceptable quality. However, the file is still a sizable 46KB.

9 Now return to the collection of images described in step 7. Turn the background off. Since the images were merged into one layer in step 7, you have to first make a selection around each one using the *Rectangular Marquee* tool. Start with the flower: Select *Copy* from the *Edit* menu and paste it into a new document.

10 Select *File>Save for Web*. Click on the *Eyedropper Color*. Ensure it is the same as the background. Select *JPEG* from the *Matte* drop-down menu. A matte is a tiny fringe of background color that is added to an image and smoothing the transition between a transparent image and the background color. Choose *Eyedropper Color*. This adds the background color to the image preview. Drag the *Quality* slider until the minimum acceptable value is reached; in our case, it was 60. Click *OK*. Repeat with the other flowers and continue with the other photos. As these are squared-up images, you can reset *Matte* to *None*.

UPLOADING AND ASSEMBLING WEB PAGES IN PAGEBUILDER

11 Connect to the Internet and sign in to Yahoo! GeoCities PageBuilder, as described on page 132. When the PageBuilder page displays, select *FileManager* from the *File* menu. With the *Images* tab selected, click the *Upload* button and *Browse* to select all the image files saved above.

12 Return to the main PageBuilder window and select *New* from the *File* menu. Then pick *Basics>Background* from the *Insert* menu and choose the background image. Click *OK*. The image then appears in the PageBuilder window.

continued ▶▶

13 Now click on the *Pictures* button and select the bride and groom image from the *User Files* menu. Drag it to the required position.

14 Select *Page Properties* from the *Format* menu and give the page a name. This is the name that appears in the browser. Since it is not a file name, spaces may be used. In the *Page Size* box, check *Layered HTML* (this enables image overlaps) and increase the *Width* to 800 pixels. This is the width visible in the PageBuilder window.

15 The extra width is now visible. Use the *Text* button to create new text blocks and write the description below the photo. We used Times Roman Italic 14 (+1) size in white. For the navigation list on the left, we used Arial Bold 10 (-1) size in black. Save this page with the name "index."

16 From the *File* menu, select *Save As* to make a copy of the page and name this one page 2. Repeat the process, this time saving it as page 3. Although we have seven links in the navigation list for this project, we have created only three pages. You can create as many pages as you require using this method.

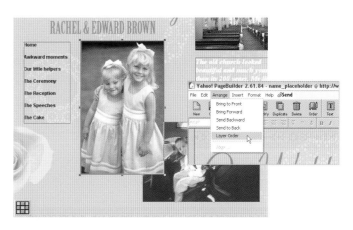

17 Open page 2, which you have just created. Insert the new images and text. We have overlapped two of the photos. When you have finished page 2, save it and then open page 3. Repeat the process of adding images and text. If you are unsure which page you are editing, the file name appears bottom left of the PageBuilder window.

18 The overlap is dictated by the order in which you insert the images. If you wish, this can be changed. Select the image that you wish to be on top and then choose *Layer Order* from the *Arrange* menu.

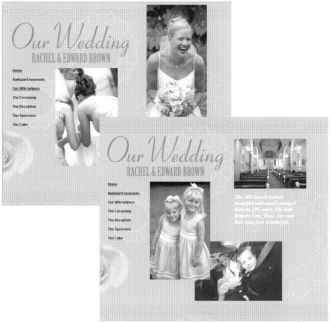

19 The final task is to add links to the text of the navigation list. First select the text. Then click the *Link* button and choose *My Page*. From the *Pick File* palette, choose the appropriate page and click *OK*. This process will have to be repeated for each link on each page. Don't forget to save the page each time before you open a new one.

20 Now you should be able to see the final result as the three pages appear in the browser. The frieze can just be seen again at the bottom of each page. This is due to the tiling of the background image.

building a vacation website

Our vacations provide us with memories that we want to treasure and share. Here we show you how to build a website that contains all those precious moments that family and friends can view—wherever they are.

To begin, download the master file template Vacation album plain.psd from the Web-linked website (*see page 166*)—you'll notice it's the same template we used to create the vacation album on page 64. By creating both a print- and screen-based version of your vacation, you will get the maximum mileage out of your holiday photos. We have also included a simple animation that you can easily recreate using the image that we have provided. Alternatively, you could use your own image.

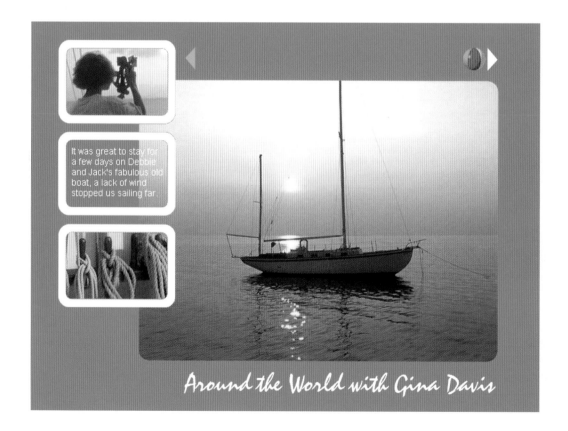

It was great to stay for a few days on Debbie and Jack's fabulous old boat, a lack of wind stopped us sailing far.

Around the World with Gina Davis

USING THE TEMPLATE

1 Open a new document in Photoshop Elements, at a size of 1,000 x 630 pixels. This will be used to assemble the various items for the website. Next open the "vacation_album_plain.psd" document and follow the steps in the box on page 152 to create the Web-optimized "web_vacation_album.psd" template. Change the background color to blue.

2 Move the "web_vacation_album.psd" window so that it partially obscures the new document. From the *Layers* palette, select the layer named "3 Panel Plain." Click on any part of the three white-bordered panels and drag from the template document to the new. Make sure that you do not release the mouse button until you are above the new document.

3 Now select the layer named "Border Plain." Using the *Magic Wand*, click inside the lighter blue border to make a selection. Select the *Move* tool from the *Tools* palette, and drag the selected box from the old document to the new, just as you did in the previous step. Don't try to drop it in the correct position; this can be changed later. Make sure the *Magic Wand* tool is not still selected when you do this, or you will be dragging the *Marquee* selection only.

4 Move the two new layers into position, making sure the blue panel is now below the white-bordered panels. Paste in a photo that you want to use on the home page. Scale it so that it slightly overlaps the blue panel. Hide the photo layer. Reselect the blue panel layer and, using the *Magic Wand*, click on the darker blue area to select it. Next, click on your photo layer to select and reveal it. Hit *Delete*, and the unwanted parts will be removed, leaving the photo with rounded corners.

continued ▶▶

Around the World with Gina Davis

5 Press Ctrl+D to deselect the selection. Paste in the two smaller photos on a layer below the white-bordered panels. Rescale them so that they fit. There is no need to trim them to fit exactly, as the white borders will hide the corners. Create a new layer for the title. We used a white color and the font Stacatto, as it has a casual feel appropriate to the theme.

altering the template for the Web

RESAMPLING AN ELEMENTS FILE

To make "web_vacation_album.psd," open "vacation_album_plain.psd." Since the latter was created for a print project, we need to alter it for Web use. Select *Resize>Image Size* from the *Image* menu. Change resolution from 300 ppi to 72 ppi (the width will reduce to 792 pixels). Ensure that both the *Constrain Proportions* and *Resample Image* boxes are checked. Select *Save As* from the *File* menu and call it "web_vacation_album.psd."

6 Ctrl+click on the white-bordered panels layer in the *Layers* palette to select its contents, and choose *Copy* from the *Edit* menu. Now select *New* from the *File* menu and paste the image into the new document. Turn off the background, and the checkerboard shows the transparent areas. Select *Save for Web* from the *File* menu and choose *GIF* from the *File*

Format drop-down. Make sure the *Eyedropper Color* is set to the color that you will be using for your background. We used blue, set to R 72, G 124, B 215. Transparency should be checked so that the photos that will appear behind the white border and will show through the "window." The *Matte* selection should be *Eyedropper Color*. Click *OK*. We named this file "panels.gif."

7 Use the *Rectangular Marquee* tool to draw a selection around the title. Use *Copy Merged* from the *File* menu and paste into a new document. Select *Save for Web* from the *File* menu and choose *GIF*. *Transparency* can be unchecked; *Matte* set to *None* and *8 Colors* will suffice. Click *OK*.

8 Select the layer containing the image pasted into the document in step 4. Copy and paste it into a new document. Turn off the background. Select *Save for Web* from the *File* menu and choose *JPEG*. Once again, select *Eyedropper Color* from the *Matte* menu. This fills the space outside the rounded corners with the background color. The *Quality* value will be fine at 40, but since the file is still quite large at 28 KB, check *Progressive*. This enables the image to appear in stages when viewed over a slow Internet connection. Then click *OK*.

9 Now select the first of the small photos to appear behind the white-bordered panels. Copy the photo and paste into a new document. Select *Save for Web* from the *File* menu and again choose *JPEG*. Because this is a simple squared-up image, we don't need a Matte. As the image will be small, *Progressive* can be unchecked. Once again, the *Quality* setting is *40*. Click *OK*. Continue copying, pasting, and saving for Web all additional photos that you plan to use in this project.

continued ▶▶

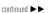

UPLOADING AND ASSEMBLING WEB PAGES

Connect to the Internet and sign in to Yahoo! GeoCities PageBuilder, as described on page 132. When the PageBuilder page displays, select *Background* from the *Format* menu and click *Set Background Color*. This is an alternative to using an image on the background. Select the color. Here, we used R 72, G 124, B 215.

Select *FileManager* from the *File* menu. With the *Images* tab selected, click the *Upload* button. Click *Browse* to select the image files saved above. When all the files have been uploaded, return to the main PageBuilder window. Click on the *Pictures* button. From the *User Files* list, select panels.gif. When it appears, drag it to the right position.

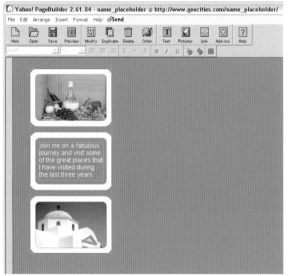

Continue by adding the two smaller photos and drag to positions on top of the white-bordered panels. They will appear above the panels. Click on the *Order* button to toggle the stacking order until the white borders appear above the photos.

Click on the *Text* button and move the resulting text box to a position within the central white border. Type in the text. We used Arial at point size 12 because a sans serif font is more readable in this situation.

Continue adding the title and the main image plus the navigation arrows *(see box at right)*. When you are satisfied with the design, select *Save* from the *File* menu. To create duplicate pages on which to base the additional pages, use *Save As* from the *File* menu and name each one. For the purpose of this project, we have created only two pages.

This is the final result as it appears in the browser. Links have been added to the arrow buttons (described in detail on page 143, step 23). The animated ball moves from left to right, rotating as it does so. At its rightmost point, it touches the arrow, which turns momentarily white.

creating animated navigation buttons

Photoshop Elements can be used to create simple animated buttons, such as the moving beach ball shown on this project. The ball was copied from the project on page 64, using the Elliptical Marquee tool to create a circular selection around it. To create the same (or similar) animated navigation button, use the following steps:

❶ Open a new document in Photoshop Elements, 110 x 37 pixels at 72 ppi. Paste in the ball and rescale it to fit. Move it to the left. Duplicate this layer three times. On each of the new layers, move the ball progressively to the right. Select *Rotate>Layer 90 degrees right* from the *Image* menu. Apply once to the second layer, twice to the third layer, and three times to the fourth.

❷ Using the *Paint Bucket,* tool, fill the transparent area of each layer with the Web page background color. We used R 72, G 124, B 215.

❸ Using the *Polygonal Lasso* tool, define an arrowhead. On layers 1, 2, and 3, use the *Paint Bucket* tool to fill with a blue to match the lighter blue in the ball. On layer 4, fill with white.

❹ Select *Save for Web* from the *File* menu and choose *GIF.* Select *Diffusion* from the *Dither* menu. Dithering helps to compensate for the lack of colors that are set to 30. Make sure that you check *Animate* and *Loop.* You can check the animation frame by frame using the arrows at the bottom of the palette. Click *OK,* and the image will be saved as an animated GIF.

❺ Finally, create an arrow facing the opposite direction (back). Using *Save for Web,* save this as a normal GIF, since it is not animated. Remember to upload these files to PageBuilder along with those described in step 12.

reference

We started this book using the description of a shoe box as the place where many conventional photographs end up. Millions of digital pictures, too, seem to be sharing the same fate, ending up on hard disks everywhere, unseen and unshared with others. I hope that by now you are convinced that your digital photo collection should not share the same fate. There are so many ways to present digital photos and, of course, to showcase them for friends and family. This section describes some of the options available, as well as showing you some of the templates you can download from the website. Also in this section we've listed website addresses that we think would be useful and tips on how to mount and frame your images if you'd like to display them.

IN THIS CHAPTER . . .

online communities and groups

Online communities enable people with common hobbies, pastimes, and interests to share them with others. You may enjoy growing cacti or coaching a local basketball team, for example. Sharing your knowledge and opinions and, in particular, your photographs online can be rewarding and worthwhile. As there are existing communities for the majority of activities, most people join one of these. If you prefer, you can create one from scratch. Most groups include facilities like chat rooms and message boards, but you need only participate in the areas that are of interest to you.

Microsoft's MSN Groups is probably the largest online community and offers free space on its website. After you have registered, you can upload your photos into an online album that is visible to all. If you create your own group, you can stipulate how access to it is granted. MSN Groups offer three categories of access:

Public: Anyone may view and become a member of this group without the permission of the manager.

Public Restricted: Anyone may view this group but needs to be approved by the manager to join.

Private: No one can view this group without first applying and being approved for membership by the manager.

A private group lets you restrict access to friends and relatives, if, for example, you want to collaborate on a family history photo album.

There are other online communities like AOL Groups and Yahoo! Groups, which are similar to MSN. Many photography manufacturers have sites dedicated to sharing photos online, too.

A TYPICAL ONLINE GROUP

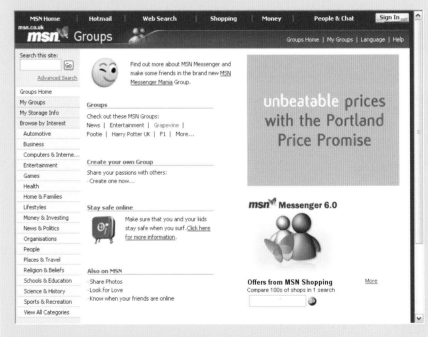

▲ The MSN Groups home page shows the group(s) that you have already created (My Groups), along with a list of categories for other groups that you might be interested in visiting or joining.

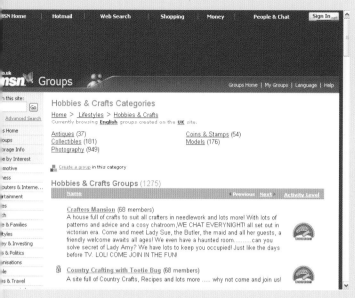

▲ The Lifestyles Group includes a Hobbies and Crafts section; photography is the most popular. The Homes and Families Group includes Family Photos and Pets.

▲ We set up our own group dedicated to our new golden retriever puppy called Monty. We have chosen to make this a public restricted group so that anyone may view Monty's photo album.

▲ Within the Photography Group is the popular digital photography club, where members can share their online photo albums.

▲ As we are the managers of the "Monty our puppy" Group, we can administer our photo album, adding new photos as Monty gets older.

professional printing options

There are a variety of professional printing services available; each one serves a particular need. You can upload your photos to an online printing service and have the prints mailed back to you in a few days. You can take your camera's memory card or make a CD of the photos and take either of these to a local store/shop where they will print them out, usually in a few hours. This service is similar to conventional photo printing, but without the film. You may want to have a T-shirt printed professionally, or perhaps a large poster. These services are also available from online suppliers.

To get the best out of any paid-for service, it is most important to supply the photos correctly. They should normally be JPEG format and any photographic enhancements made beforehand (*see pages 26–37*). The size of your original photo will dictate the maximum print size (*see chart*). Do not use the *Save for Web* option to optimize your photos, as this is reserved for images that will only appear onscreen. Simply use *Save As* and select *JPEG*. Choose *Maximum Quality (12)* but leave the other options at the default settings. If your original photos are high-quality, they can of course be used straight from the camera.

A list of online printing providers is given on page 166.

getting technical

Photos size options

Image Resolution In pixels	Maximum Print Size Very Good Quality	Maximum Print Size Best Quality
512 x 384	Wallets (2.1" x 3.1") [5.3 x 7.9 cm]	Wallets (2.1" x 3.1") [5.3 x 7.9 cm]
640 x 480	3.5" x 5" or 4" x 6" (9 x 13 cm or 10 x 15 cm)	Wallets (2.1" x 3.1") [5.3 x 7.9 cm]
800 x 600	5" x 7" (13 x 18 cm)	3.5" x 5" (9 x 13 cm)
1,024 x 768	8" x 10" (20 x 25 cm)	4" x 6" (10 x 15 cm)
1,152 x 864	8" x 12" (20 x 30.5 cm)	5" x 7" (13 x 18 cm)
1,536 x 1,024	11" x 14" (28 x 35.5 cm)	8" x 10" (20 x 25 cm)
1,600 x 1,200	11" x 14" (28 x 35.5 cm)	8" x 12" (20 x 30.5 cm)
1,712 x 1,368	16" x 20" (40.5 x 51 cm)	11" x 14" (28 x 35.5 cm)
2,048 x 1,536	20" x 30" (51 x 76 cm)	16" x 20" (40.5 x 51 cm)
2,400 x 1,800	20" x 30" (51 x 76 cm)	20" x 30" (51 x 76 cm)

ONLINE PRINTING SERVICES

▲ A provider such as Printroom.com enables you to upload photos and then select from a range of special printing options.

▲ Using this facility, you can store your photos indefinitely so they can be viewed online. You can also use the service to print photos whenever you wish.

▲ Fuji offers all the options: You can upload photos for online printing; take them to a local photo print store, or Fuji's Aladdin kiosk to add borders and color, crop pictures, and rotate shots before ordering the prints.

▲ Small independent providers such as anyTime Photo offer similar services—storing and printing your photos.

continued ▶▶

1-Click Photo

| Import | Organize and Archive | Enhance | Make a Book | Share Online | Prints |

As the majority of consumers bypass traditional film cameras in favor of digital photography, an impressive number of them have insisted on being able to continue to enjoy one of the few remaining benefits of film — the ability to order prints. And here too, digital photography has a significant advantage over film: it gives you the option to order high-quality prints selectively (that is, having prints made only of those pictures that turn out the way you like).

iPhoto in action

Order Prints - Order prints from Kodak delivered in One-Click.

Printer Compatibility

iPhoto supports digital cameras from the companies listed below. For a list of which models are supported, check out the printer compatibility page.

- Apple
- Canon
- Epson
- HP
- Lexmark
- Xerox/Techtronix

Convenient prints

Order Prints — Apple recognized this phenomenon early on in the digital revolution, which is why iPhoto users have always been able to order glossy prints and professionally-bound photo albums directly from the application. And now iPhoto 2 comes with even more printing and print-ordering options.

Fact is, if you have a color printer, you can print high-quality photos right from the comfort of your own home. iPhoto enables you to output high-quality color prints in a variety of standard photo sizes and formats, including custom greeting cards and contact sheets, right to your printer. iPhoto 2 provides an easy to follow menu of printing presets — such as Glossy-Normal and Matte-Fine — for many popular inkjet printers, making printing great photos as simple as choosing from a few standard settings and hitting the Print button. And because iPhoto 2 comes with additional printing templates — yes, even in the perennially popular

Contact Sheet | Full Page | Greeting Card

▲ Nearly all the online services are available to either PC or Mac users. Currently Apple offers a service available only to Mac users since it is accessed using the Macintosh iPhoto application. Mac users might prefer it even though the service is limited.

4x6 Prints only 25¢ | Log In | Help

| Join Now | Buy Prints | Buy Gifts & Cards | Gallery | Album Search | Tools

BIG Print Center

Make a *big hit* with your photos!

Home > Our Store > Big Print Cen...

We are proud to offer you our state-of-the-art digital and film image printing services for your large prints. We offer BIGGER and BETTER services that tower over the rest!

Professional-Quality Photo at Prices Made for You!

Our photo lab uses a LightJet photo printer for your poster size prints. This is the same quality printer used by the top-tier professional processing labs around the world. Our printer can produce museum-quality prints equivalent to 3000 dpi print resolution. The LightJet uses laser exposure on photographic paper so our fade-resistant prints can last for decades! You can create prints of multiple sizes, as wide as 40". The results are professional quality prints that will have excellent contrast, rich color rendition, deep blacks, radiant whites and razor sharp prints.

Our Advantages

- Any size prints up to 40" wide
- Professional Kodak Paper
- Museum-quality prints equivalent to 3000 dpi
- Your choice of photographic or inkjet prints
- All formats available in either Matte or Glossy finish
- Fast Service and Delivery

Our professional photo prints are ideal for Wedding photos, Portraits, School Photos, Posters and Wall hangings and more!

Canvas Prints

We also offer, using a different technology than above,

30x40 ($39.95)
24x36 ($26.95)
20x30 ($18.95)
20x24 ($17.95)
18x24 ($16.95)
20x20 ($14.95)
16x24 ($14.95)
16x20 ($13.95)
12x18 ($10.95)

We Use Kodak PAPER Turn up the Color

Make a BIG hit!

Photo Selection:
Click on the image below to change your selected photo.

⚠ Image doesn't meet the minimum recommended resolution. Please refer to this product's specifications.

Resolution: 2400 x 1600

Product	Price	Quantity
Gloss Photo Poster 12 x 18"	$10.95	
Gloss Photo Poster 16 x 20"	$13.95	
Gloss Photo Poster 16 x 24"	$14.95	
Gloss Photo Poster 20 x 20"	$14.95	
Gloss Photo Poster 18 x 24"	$16.95	
Gloss Photo Poster 20 x 24"	$17.95	
Gloss Photo Poster 20 x 30"	$18.95	
Gloss Photo Poster 24 x 36"	$26.95	
Gloss Photo Poster 30 x 40"	$39.95	⚠
Lustre Photo Poster 12 x 18"	$10.95	
Lustre Photo Poster 16 x 20"	$13.95	

▲ Large-format printing is also available online. However, unless your image is very high resolution, the results are likely to be disappointing. A reputable provider like this one will alert you to the fact that even this 2,400 x 1,600-pixel photo doesn't meet the minimum requirement for a 30 x 40-in. (76 x 100-cm) print.

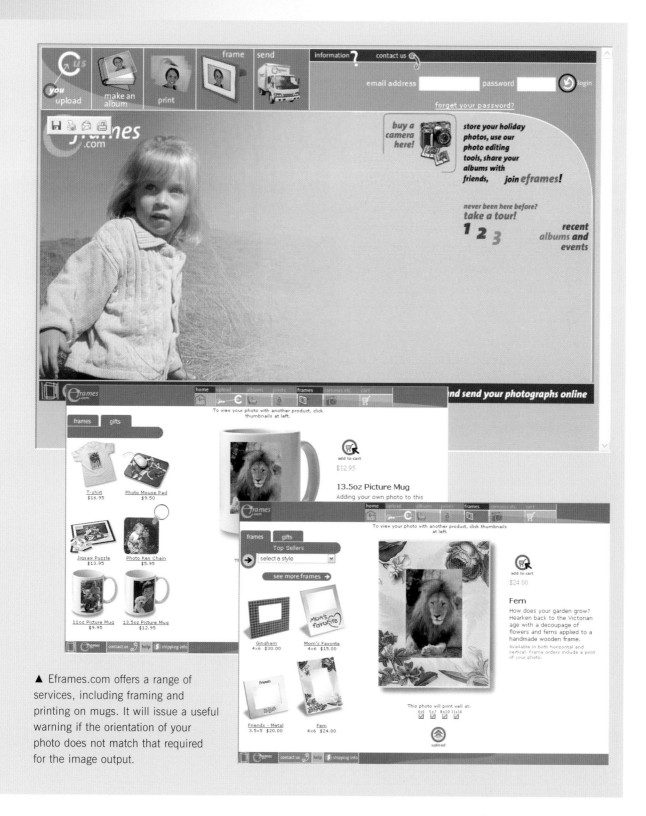

▲ Eframes.com offers a range of services, including framing and printing on mugs. It will issue a useful warning if the orientation of your photo does not match that required for the image output.

borders and backgrounds

In addition to the images we have provided, you can find borders and backgrounds in many different places. Choose from greeting cards, wrapping paper, wallpaper, packaging, old books and magazines, or scanned objects like leaves or lace. Some books provide royalty-free scannable images for domestic use. Other sources are clip art supplied with some software packages and also available to download from the Internet. Applications such as Photoshop Elements also have tools to help you create repeat patterns and decorative borders.

The images on this page can be downloaded from the Web-linked website (www.prdpus.web-linked.com). If you prefer to scan the images on these pages, set the scanner to grayscale, scale to 100% and the resolution to 600 ppi.

Vacation album (*see page 64*)

Wedding album
(*see page 144*)

Wedding album (*see page 144*)

Floral frame
(*see page 69*)

Family tree
(*see page 72*)

T-shirt border
(*see page 95*)

Chrome frame
(*see page 71*)

useful Web links

We hope that *How to Do Just about Anything with Your Digital Photos* has provided inspiration as well as instruction, and that you are now set to take advantage of the myriad service and information providers that are available on the Web. The links listed here are all available from our Web-linked site, so you do not need to type them into your browser. The site address is www.prdpus.web-linked.com; there you'll also find all of the templates referred to in various projects throughout the book.

Digital photo printing services

USA, Canada, and Pacific Rim	Web address
AGFAnet Print Service	www.agfanet.com
Apple iPhoto, Cupertino, CA	www.apple.com/ilife/iphoto
Burch's One Hour Photo, Kalispell and Whitefish, MT	www.kalispellphoto.com
dotPhoto Inc., West Trenton, NJ	www.dotphoto.com
eFrames.com, St. Cloud, FL	www.eFrames.com
Fotki.com, New York, NY	www.fotki.com
Fromex Photo Lab, Long Beach, CA	www.fromex.com
Fuji DigitalCameraDeveloping.com	www.digitalcameradeveloping.com
ImageStation.com (Sony Electronics), San Jose, CA	www.imagestation.com
Ofoto Inc. (a Kodak Company), Emeryville, CA	www.ofoto.com
OurPictures, Palo Alto, CA	www.ourpictures.com
PhotoFun.com, Scottsdale, AZ	www.photofun.com
PhotoAccess Corporation, Seattle, WA	www.photoaccess.com
Shutterfly, Redwood City, CA	www.shutterfly.com
Snapfish, San Francisco, CA	www.snapfish.com
WebPhotos.com, Gaithersburg, MD	www.webphotos.com
Carsand-Mosher Photographic, Nova Scotia	www.carsandmosher.ca
Future Photo, Alberta/B.C./Ontario/Quebec	pix.futureshop.ca
Japan Camera, Canada	www.japancamera.com
London Drugs Company, Alberta/B.C./Manitoba/Saskatchewan	www.ldphotostation.com
Kodak Express, Philippines	www.kodakexpress.com.ph
FrogPrints, Auckland, New Zealand	www.frogprints.co.nz
National Photos (Kodak Australiasia), Moorebank, NSW, Australia	www.kodakdirect.com.au
Print@Fujicolor, Brookvale NSW, Australia	www.fujicolor.com.au
Universal Photo Factory, Toronto NSW, Australia	www.bgnphotography.com.au

Specialist printing services

	Web address
Eshirt (wear your ideas)	**www.eshirt.it**

Online photo-sharing services

AGFAnet Slideshow	**www.agfanet.com**
Freeserve Photos	**http://photos.freeserve.com**
Kodak Online	**www.kodak.com**
MSN Photos	**http://photos.msn.com**
Sony ImageStation	**www.imagestation.com**
Subscription Central (MSN Photos Plus)	**http://join.msn.com**

Online printing advice and reference

Online printing expert	**http://online-printing-expert.com**
Digital Imaging Florida University	**www.fsu.edu/~dmpg/imaging**
Envelope sizes	**www.envelope.org**
EXIF.org	**www.exif.org**
Folex AG	**www.folex.ch**
The Myth of DPI	**www.rideau-info.com/genealogy/digital/dpi.html**

Digital cameras and scanner information

Digital Cameras on creativepro.com	**www.creativepro.com**
Scanner Reviews	**www.imaging-resource.com/SCAN1.HTM**
DP review	**www.dpreview.com**
The Imaging Resource Guide to Desktop Scanners	**www.imaging-resource.com/ARTS/SCANG/SCANG.HTM**

Web page builders and image galleries

Web Image Gallery Creation Tools	**http://graphicssoft.about.com/cs/webgallery**
Yahoo! GeoCities	**http://geocities.yahoo.com**
Official Yahoo! PageBuilder Help	**http://help.yahoo.com/help/us/geo/builder**
Yahoo! PageBuilder Help Site	**http://www.yahoopagebuilderhelp.com**
Yahoo! PageBuilder	**http://geocities.yahoo.com/v/pb.html**
Yahoo! SiteBuilder	**http://webhosting.yahoo.com/ps/sb**
Link to sample home page	**http://www.geocities.com/name_placeholder**

trimming, pasting, and painting

Although this book is primarily concerned with digital solutions for presenting your photos, there may come a time when the old-fashioned cut-and-paste methods are needed to provide the finishing touches. By pasting together prints, you will be able to overcome the size limitations of your desktop printer. Finally, painting over your photos with acrylic paints or glitter pens can create fun and decorative touches that have a real hand-made feel.

You can also apply digital images directly onto household surfaces. For example, you could ring a nursery wall with a border of adorable puppies or decorate an old cabinet with photos of family celebrations. Since most inkjet prints are made from water-soluble inks, it is essential to first apply a fixative coating spray, available from most art stores. The list below shows useful equipment. Preparation is usually the key to success, along with your creativity.

What you'll need for:

Trimming
• A sharp craft knife. Used together with a steel rule (below), a craft knife is essential for making long, straight cuts.
• A steel rule. Don't use a plastic rule, since you'll find the blade of the knife can slip over the edge of the rule and may cut your fingers.
• A purpose-made cutting mat. This provides a stable surface on which to cut out your photos. A sheet of stout card will do, but you'll find you have to replace it after you've used it several times.
• Slender scissors. Ideal for cutting around difficult shapes.
• Dressmakers' pinking shears. Useful for cutting wavy edges.

Pasting
• Adhesive sprays. This type of adhesive is best for mounting photographs. However, they are not sold in some areas due to the health risk if they are inhaled. Always use adhesive sprays in a well-ventilated area and follow the manufacturer's instructions.
• Water-based adhesive. This type of adhesive is good for sturdier materials.

• Double-sided tape. This type of sticky tape can be effective, but it doesn't offer a second chance if an element of your presentation is incorrectly placed.
• Adhesive sticks. These are useful for covering large areas but can be difficult to control and sometimes leave globules of unwanted glue.
• Glue guns. Ideal for sticking really chunky objects.
• Small roller. When using any type of adhesive we recommend that you use a roller rather than pressing glued surfaces together by hand.

Painting
• Glitter/gel pens. As most of your images will be created digitally, these types of pen leave a three-dimensional trail, and create a really hand-made finish. Nail polish can also be used to create discrete blobs.
• Acrylic/oil paints. Such paints can be used to create a textured surface, but be prepared to allow for the drying time.
• Gold/silver metallic paints. These create a finish that a computer cannot replicate.
• Gilt wax. This can be difficult to handle but if used carefully can give many surfaces a touch of splendor.

framing your photos

As we have seen in a number of projects in this book, it's very easy to create an effective "virtual" frame using software like Photoshop Elements, or by photographing or scanning real frames and borders to use with your digital photographs. However, if you really want to show off your images and hang them on the walls in your home or give them as gifts, then a real frame is the best option.

Deciding whether to make or purchase your frame (and liner or mat if necessary) is your first step. Next, it's important to arrange the project so that it fits within the frame when printed. With rectangular frames, this is easy to do, but with some highly decorative frames—an Art Nouveau design, for example—the image may appear behind an irregular shape. If you buy a new frame, it will almost certainly have a sample print inside that can be used as a guide. If this is not the case, try scanning the frame, scale the image to match it, and then discard the scanned frame before printing.

If your skills extend to making things, why not buy the molding and make the frame yourself? Make sure that you cut the corners with a miter saw. You could also decorate a plain, unmolded frame with seashells or create a decorative border from modeling clay or salt dough.

A few rules of thumb:

❶ Don't put a project that uses a virtual frame into a real one: frames within frames are not attractive; use a borderless glass frame instead.

❷ Match the character of the image with a suitable framing material; for example, dignified hardwood for seniors; silver for newlyweds; plastic for kids.

❸ Use a multi-opening frame to record events like a wedding or phases of a child's life such as the first day of school, receiving a sports award, or a school prom.

❹ Always match the print to the actual frame size. An oversized image shoe-horned into a small frame or a small image lost in a vast frame look equally bad.

glossary

Adobe Inc. Software developer whose products are widely used by professionals and amateurs for many creative tasks such as Web design, graphic design and video editing. Photoshop, Photoshop Elements, Photoshop Album and the video-editing package Premiere are some of its most successful products.

alpha channel While each color channel defines the level of a certain color for each pixel, this channel defines the level of transparency for each pixel, allowing you to create images with objects of varying levels of transparency.

anti-aliasing The smoothing of jagged edges on diagonal lines created in an imaging program by giving intermediate values to pixels between the steps. This is especially common around text.

application Software designed to make the computer perform a specific task. For example, Photoshop is an image-editing application, whereas Windows is an operating system.

artifact Any flaw in a digital image, such as "noise." Most artifacts are undesirable, although adding "noise" can create a desirable grainy texture if an image is appropriate.

back-up A copy of either a file or a program created in case the original file becomes damaged (corrupt) or lost.

bit depth The number of bits per pixel (usually per channel, sometimes for all the channels combined), which determines the number of colors that pixels can display. Eight bits-per-channel are needed for photographic-quality imaging.

bitmapped graphic An image made up of dots, or pixels, such as those produced by digital cameras, scanners, and software like Photoshop. It is distinct from the vector images of "object-oriented" drawing applications.

browser/Web browser Program that enables the viewing or "browsing" of World Wide Web pages across the Internet. The most widely used browsers are Netscape Navigator and Microsoft Internet Explorer.

burn(ing) The act of recording data onto a CD using a CD burner (a recordable CD drive). Software such as Ahead Nero (PC) or Roxio's Toast (Mac) is often used for this task.

byte Eight bits—the basic data unit of desktop computing.

CCD (Charged Coupled Device) The name given to the component of a digital camera that "sees" and records the images, like film does in a traditional camera. The CCD is made up of a grid of tiny light sensors, one for each pixel. The number of sensors, and the size of image output by the CCD are measured in megapixels.

CD-ROM CD (Compact Disk) Read-Only Memory. An evolution of the CD that allows the storage of up to 600 megabytes of data, such as images, video clips, text and other digital files. But the disks are "Read only," which means the user can't edit or overwrite the data.

CD-R/CD-RW CD Recordable/CD-ReWriteable. CD-Rs are inexpensive disks on which you can store any digital data, or roughly 77 minutes of audio (on a hi-fi CD recorder). But once written and finalized (fixed), the data cannot be erased, edited, or modified. Similar to the above, CD-RW disks can be "unfinalized," then overwritten, in part or entirely, any number of times. However, CD-RWs will not play on all CD drives, so they are primarily used for storage.

channel Images are commonly described in terms of channels, which can be viewed as a sheet of color similar to a layer. Commonly, a color image will have a channel allocated to each primary color (red, green, and blue in a standard RGB image) and sometimes an alpha channel for transparency, or even an additional channel for professional printing with special inks.

clone/cloning In most image-editing packages, clone tools allow the user to sample pixels (picture elements) from one part of an image, such as a digital photograph, and use them to "paint" over another area of the image. This process is often used for the removal of unwanted parts of an image or correcting problems, such as facial blemishes. In Photoshop, the tool is called the Clone Stamp tool (sometimes known as the rubber stamp).

CMYK The standard primary colors used by professional, or "process," printing: cyan, magenta, yellow, and key (black). These colors are mixed according to "subtractive color," meaning that white appears where no color value is applied.

color depth See bit depth.

color gamut The range of color that can be produced by an output device, such as a printer, a monitor, or a film recorder.

color picker An on-screen palette of colors used to describe and define the colors displayed and used in an application or on a computer monitor. Color pickers may be specific to an application such as Adobe Photoshop, a third-party color system such as PANTONE, or to the operating system running on your computer.

compression The technique of rearranging data so that it either occupies less space on a disk or transfers faster between devices or over communication lines. For example, high-quality digital images, such as photographs, can take up an enormous amount of disk space, transfer slowly, and use a lot of processing power. They need to be compressed (the file size needs to be made smaller) before they can be published on the Web: Otherwise they take too long to appear on-screen. But compressing them can lead to a loss of quality. Compression methods that do not lose data are referred to as "lossless," while "lossy" describes methods in which some data are lost.

continuous-tone image An image, such as a photograph, in which there is a smooth progression of tones from black to white.

contrast The degree of difference between adjacent tones in an image from the lightest to the darkest. "High contrast" describes an image with light highlights and dark shadows, but few shades in between, while a "low contrast" image is one with even tones and few dark areas or highlights.

copyright The right of a person who creates an original work to protect that work by controlling how and where it may be reproduced.

copyright-free A misnomer used to describe ready-made resources, such as clip art. In fact, these resources are rarely, if ever, "copyright free." Generally it is only the license to use the material that is granted by purchase. "Royalty free" is a more accurate description, since you don't have to pay per copy used.

digitize To convert anything—text, images, or sound—into binary form so that it can be digitally processed. In other words, transforming analog data (a traditional photograph or an audio tape, for example) into digital data.

dithering A technique by which a large range of colors can be simulated by mingling pixels. A complex pattern of intermingling adjacent pixels of two colors gives the illusion of a third color, although this makes the image appear grainy.

dots per inch (dpi) A unit of measurement used to represent the resolution of output devices such as printers and also, erroneously, monitors and images, whose resolution should be expressed in pixels per inch (ppi). The closer the dots or pixels (the more there are to each inch) the better the quality. Typical resolutions are 72 ppi for a monitor, 600 dpi for a laser printer, and 1,440 dpi for an inkjet printer.

download To transfer data from a remote computer, such as an Internet server, to your own. The opposite of upload.

DVD (Digital Versatile Disk). Similar in appearance to CDs and CD-ROMs, but with a much greater storage capacity. Although store-bought movie DVDs hold up to 18 GB, you can burn only around 4–5 GB on the various home formats. Like CD-R and CD-RW you can get blank disks that can be written once or rewritten repeatedly. Unlike CDs, however, there are competing formats that look the same but cannot write to each other's disks. These are DVD-R/RW, DVD+R/RW, and DVD-RAM. When buying blank disks, be sure to get the correct type. The write-once disks from both DVD-R and DVD+R can be read by most modern DVD players so, with the correct software, you can make DVDs of photo slide shows or digital videos at home.

EPS (Encapsulated PostScript) Image file format for object-oriented graphics, as in drawing programs and page-layout programs.

extract A process in many image-editing applications whereby a selected part of an image is removed from areas around it. Typically, a subject is "extracted" from the background.

eyedropper tool In some applications, a tool for gauging the color of adjacent pixels.

file extension The term for the abbreviated suffix at the end of a file name that describes either its type (such as .eps or .jpg) or origin (the application that created it, such as .qxp for QuarkXPress files). Extensions are compulsory and essentially automatic in Windows, but not on Apple computers, so Mac users should add them if they want their files to work on Windows computers.

file format The way a program arranges data so that it can be stored or displayed on a computer. Common file formats include TIFF (.tif) and JPEG (.jpg) for bitmapped image files, EPS (.eps) for object-oriented image files, and ASCII (.txt) for text files.

FireWire A type of port connection that allows for high-speed transfer of data between a computer and peripheral devices. Also known as IEEE-1394 or iLink, this method of transfer—quick enough for digital video—is employed by some high-resolution cameras to move data faster than USB.

frame A single still picture from a movie or animation sequence. Also a single complete image from a TV picture.

font Set of characters sharing the same typeface; these are stored by your computer and made available to applications where text is edited. There are two varieties of fonts; vector fonts like TrueType that can be printed at any size with no loss of quality, and bitmapped fonts, which cannot be scaled.

GB (gigabyte) Approximately one billion bytes (actually 1,073,741,824), or 1,024 megabytes.

GIF (Graphics Interchange Format) One of the main bitmapped image formats used on the Internet. GIF is a 256-color format with two specifications, GIF87a and, more recently, GIF89a, the latter providing additional features such as the use of transparent backgrounds. The GIF format uses a "lossless" compression technique, which handles areas of similar color well and allows animation. It is therefore the most common format for graphics and logos on the Internet, but JPEG is preferred for photographs.

gradation/gradient The smooth transition from one color or tone to another. Photoshop and other programs include a Gradient tool to create these transitions automatically.

histogram A "map" of the distribution of tones in an image, arranged as a graph. The horizontal axis is in 256 steps from black to white (or dark to light), and the vertical axis is the number of pixels, so in a dark image you'll find taller bars in the darker shades.

HSL (Hue, Saturation, Lightness) A way of representing colors based upon the way that colors are transmitted from a TV screen or monitor. The hue is the pure color from the spectrum, the saturation is the intensity of the color pigment (without black or white added), and lightness represents the strength of luminance from light to dark (the amount of black or white present). Variously called HLS (hue, lightness, saturation), HSV (hue, saturation, value) and HSB (hue, saturation, brightness).

hue A color found in its pure state in the spectrum.

icon An on-screen graphical representation of an object (such as a disk, file, or folder), tool, or feature, used to make identification and selection easier.

interface A term used to describe the screen design that links the user with the computer program or website. The quality of the user interface often determines how well users will be able to navigate their way around the pages within the site.

interpolation Bitmapping procedure used in resizing an image to maintain resolution. When the number of pixels is increased, interpolation fills in the gaps by comparing the values of adjacent pixels.

ISP (Internet Service Provider) An organization that provides access to the Internet. At its most basic this may be a telephone number for connection, but most ISPs provide email addresses and Web space for new sites.

JPEG (The Joint Photographic Experts Group) An ISO (International Standards Organization) group that defines compression standards for bitmapped color images. The abbreviated form gives its name to a "lossy" (meaning some data may be lost) compressed file format in which the degree of compression, ranging from high compression and low quality, to low compression and high quality, can be defined by the user.

KB (kilobyte) Approximately 1,000 bytes (actually 1,024).

lasso tool A selection tool used to draw an outline around an area.

layer One level of an image file, separate from the rest, allowing different elements to be moved and edited in much the same way as animators draw onto sheets of transparent acetate.

lossless/lossy Refers to the data-losing qualities of different compression methods. "Lossless" means that no image information is lost; "lossy" means that some (or much) of the image data are lost in the compression process (but the data will download more quickly).

luminosity Brightness of color. This does not affect the hue or color saturation.

mask A grayscale template that hides part of an image. One of the most important tools in editing an image, it is used to make changes to a limited area. In Photoshop Elements a mask can be applied only to an adjustment layer, but in Photoshop masks can be applied to all layers.

MB (megabyte) Approximately one million bytes (actually 1,048,576).

megapixel This has become the typical measure of the resolution of a digital camera's CCD. It is simply the number of pixels on the CCD, so a size of 1,280 x 960 pixels is equal to 1,228,800 pixels, or 1.2 megapixels.

memory card The media employed by a digital camera for saving photos. This can be Compact Flash, Memory Stick, SD Cards or Smart Media—all store images that can then be transferred to the computer.

menu An on-screen list of choices available to the user.

midtones/middletones The range of tonal values in an image anywhere between the darkest and lightest, usually referring to those approximately halfway.

noise Random pattern of small spots on a digital image that are generally unwanted, caused by non-image-forming electrical signals. Noise is a type of artifact.

pixel (picture element) The smallest component of any digitally generated image. In its simplest form, one pixel corresponds to a single bit: 0 = off, or white, and 1 = on, or black. In color or grayscale images or monitors, one pixel may correspond to several bits. An 8-bit pixel, for example, can be displayed in any of 256 colors, a 24-bit pixel (8 bits per channel) can display any one of 16.8 million colors.

pixels per inch (ppi) A measure of resolution for a bitmapped image.

plug-in Subsidiary software for a browser or other package that enables it to perform additional functions; e.g., play sound, movies, or video.

PNG (Portable Network Graphics) A file format for images used on the Web, which provides 10–30% "lossless" compression, or a "lossy" option. It was created as an alternative to the GIF and JPG file formats, but has not yet displaced either.

RAM (Random Access Memory) The working memory of a computer, to which the central processing unit (CPU) has direct, immediate access. The data here are stored only while the computer is switched on; and more RAM can dramatically improve a computer's performance.

raster(ization) Derived from the Latin word "rastrum," meaning "rake," this is the method of displaying (and creating) images on a television or computer screen. It is commonly used to mean the conversion of a scalable vector graphics image into a bitmapped image.

resampling Changing the resolution of an image either by removing pixels (lowering the resolution) or adding them by interpolation (increasing the resolution).

resolution (1) The degree of quality, definition, or clarity with which an image is reproduced or displayed; for example, in a photograph or via a scanner, monitor screen, printer, or other output device.

resolution (2) Monitor resolution, screen resolution. The number of pixels across by pixels down. Common resolutions are 640 x 480, 800 x 600, and 1,024 x 768, with 800 x 600 the size most Web designers plan for.

RGB (Red, Green, Blue) The primary colors of the "additive" color model, used in video technology, computer monitors, and for graphics such as for the Web and multimedia.

ROM (Read-Only Memory) Memory, such as on a CD-ROM, which can only be read, not written to. It retains its contents without power, unlike RAM.

rubber stamp Another word for a clone tool (see cloning).

software Programs that enable a computer to perform tasks, from its operating system to job-specific applications such as image-editing programs and third-party filters.

thumbnail A small representation of an image used mainly for identification purposes in a file browser or, within Photoshop, to illustrate the current status of layers and channels.

TIFF (Tagged Image File Format) A standard and popular graphics file format originally developed by Aldus (now merged with Adobe) and Microsoft. It is used for scanned, high-resolution, bitmapped images and for color separations. The TIFF format stores each pixel's color individually, with no compression, at whatever bit depth you choose. That means they can be black and white, grayscale, RGB color, or CMYK color, can be read by different computer platforms, but can be very large files. For example, an image of 640 x 480 pixels (just 0.3 megapixels) at 8 bits per channel CMYK (32 bits per pixel) is 1.2 MB.

tile, tiling Repeating a graphic item and placing the repetitions side-by-side in all directions so that they form a pattern.

toolbox In an application, an area of the interface that enables instant access to the most commonly used commands and features. Unless switched off by the user, the toolbox is always visible on-screen.

transparency A degree of transparency applied to a pixel so that, when the image or layer is used in conjunction with others, it can be seen through. Only some file formats allow for transparency, including TIFFs, which define transparency as an alpha channel, or GIFs, which allow only absolute transparency (a pixel is either colored or transparent).

TrueType A type of font or typeface composed of vector graphics that can be scaled up or down without any loss in quality.

USB (Universal Serial Bus) An interface standard developed to replace the slow, unreliable serial and parallel ports on computers. USB allows devices to be plugged and unplugged while the computer is switched on. It is now the standard means for connecting printers, scanners, and digital cameras.

vector graphics Images made up of mathematically defined shapes, such as circles and rectangles, or complex paths built out of mathematically defined curves. Vector graphics images can be displayed at any size or resolution without loss of quality. They are easy to edit because the shapes retain their identity, but they lack the tonal subtlety of bitmapped images. They are used in illustrations for their accuracy and clarity and are employed by Photoshop's text handling and shape tools.

Web page A published HTML document on the World Wide Web, which when linked with others, forms a website. The HTML code contains text, layout, and navigational instructions, plus links to the graphics used on the page.

Web server A computer ("host") that is dedicated to Web services.

website The address, location (on a server), and collection of documents and resources for any particular interlinked set of Web pages.

Windows Operating System for PCs developed by Microsoft using a graphic interface.

World Wide Web (WWW) The term used to describe the entire collection of Web servers all over the world that are connected to the Internet.

index

acknowledgments

There are a great many people who I would like to thank who helped in the creation of this book, but I would like to single out the unstinting support of my family and my dog Monty, for being such a patient model, and the help and understanding of the editors at ILEX.

The majority of the images used in the projects were from Photos.com, the best online photo resource around.